SHOWROOMS

BRIGITTE FITOUSSI

PRINCETON ARCHITECTURAL PRESS

Born in Tunis in 1956, Brigitte Fitoussi received her architectural degree in Paris in 1982. She spent the following year in Milan studying Italian design; she studied under Achille Castiglioni at the Politecnico and worked at the office of Cini Boeri. Following her return to France in 1984, she has worked at Architecture d'aujourd'hui *as editor of the feature "Design et intérieur" and has written for several other journals*: Intramuros, Elle, l'Expansion, Espace de bureau, De Diseño, Maison française, Ardi, *etc. She also consults in the area of industrial and interior design.*

The author wishes to thank the architects and photographers who generously furnished the illustrations for this book, and Architecture d'aujourd'hui, *which allowed use of its library and graciously lent photographic materials. The author also wishes to thank Valérie Vaudou, Lucette Lomband, Sylvie Deleule, Michèle Fitoussi, and Sophie Anargyros, as well as the people at Electa Moniteur, who made this project possible.*

Published in English language by
Princeton Architectural Press
37 East Seventh Street
New York, NY 10003
212.995.9620

English Translation: Lois Nesbitt
Production Editor: Clare L. Jacobson
Copy Editor: Ann C. Urban
Cover Photograph:
©T. Nakasa & Partners

Special thanks to Sheila Cohen, Antje Fritsch, and Elizabeth Short of Princeton Architectural Press.
—Kevin C. Lippert, Publisher

ISBN 0-910413-67-3

CONTENTS

SHOWROOMS IN THE 1980'S

One's first impression of a city is often influenced by its showrooms. Walking in any city, before one can apprehend the character of its houses or monuments, storefronts offer an immediate urban perception. Alike and different, sometimes isolated, often juxtaposed, they confront the on-looker. Their windows and signs send out a series of instantaneous images on the nature of the place, its style and quality of life, and finally on its inhabitants and their affluence.

Punctuating the city with their lights day and night, showrooms attract and seduce the passerby by offering multiple scenes—from the banal to the magnificent—to the theater of the street, which change according to the tastes and fashion of the season. If storefronts have changed over the centuries, they have conserved, whatever the context, their character that is unique to the city. In *Invisible Cities*, Italo Calvino writes, "If a building has neither sign nor face, its own form and the place it occupies in the order of the city suffice to indicate its function."[1]

However, from the nineteenth century, the beginning of modern times, until today, the era of communication, showrooms have not stopped evolving, surpassing more and more the simple problems of form and function. And with the beginning of the 1980's, they began to show signs of new mutations.

The era of arcades

In nineteenth-century Europe, industrialization and progress in glass technology allowed the development of a kind of showroom—now called bourgeois—characterized by a type of facade that still exists today; behind transparent windows, a more or less wide variety of neatly presented products invited the customer to come inside. During this period, while more traditional forms of commerce—booths or stalls in commercial streets and markets—continued for the less well-to-do classes, the bourgeosie created large stores and arcades, on the model of the covered streets of the Middle Ages and the Renaissance. Thus began the era of the street arcade, the rue de Rivoli and Palais Royal in Paris, Bond Street in London, and the Corso Vittorio-Emanuele in Milan, where strollers, partially protected from inclement weather, could walk while looking in the shop windows.

Forseeing the needs of the rich, stores differentiated themselves by the quality and variety of the products—gloves, perfumes, hats, shirts, chocolates, shoes, and so on—and by specific signs and displays. Nevertheless, as part of a coherent whole, they ended up resembling one another, largely due to their location under the arcades, but also because their clientele belonged to the same social class. We now live in a vastly different world, a consumer society of standardized modes of production, and yet in some ways surprisingly similar to the nineteenth century.

The era of marketing

In the twentieth century, under American influence, the commercial world has been radically transformed; it is an era of marketing and involves much more complex systems of production and distribution. Mass consumption, chain stores, franchises, supermarkets and, of course, advertising has induced changes in tastes at all levels of so-called liberal societies. Thus, the shops of this century, while continuing to perpetuate an urban and commercial tradition, have undegone changes of type, dimension, and form. Stores have multiplied in cities, to the point that their identity has been lost.

Perhaps this explains the emergence in the last ten years of an almost frantic search for trademark visibility. It is a question of up-scale, rather elitist markets attaching themselves to the distribution of manufactured goods (most often carrying designer labels) such as pret-a-porter, shoes, jewelry, objects, and home furnishings.

The era of communication

In the 1980's, a flowering of high design showrooms—conceived in perfect harmony with their contents—appeared around the world, signaling the mutations of the times.

Advertising messages are no longer carried only by signs or windows. Each product's image is researched and transmitted according to a lifestyle or repertory of tastes, to which the intended customer will hopefully identify. This is what is known in advertising terms as "global communication." In this line of thought, the architecture of the store is primary; it becomes the "medium," which communicates the culture of specific target groups rather than the merchandise. A subtle semantic: everything is sold, from the space to the packaging. These showrooms, whose configurations are increasingly subject to artistic expression as well as architecture, interior design, scenography, graphic design, audiovisual effects, and animation, are the subject of this book. These showrooms differentiate themselves from the ordinary by a more sophisticated realization or by the quality and diversity of their design, which transforms the street and the city.

Expressions and style in the 1980's
Certain of these showrooms, protected by a unique skin of glass in a metal frame, no longer have display windows. Almost slipping outside the shop, the naked interiors present superb stage sets and different sales scenarios; the entire interior is exposed, becoming itself a window.

At the same time, these showrooms are almost empty; the stock of clothes or products have disappeared in favor of a stark display. Influenced by the Japanese, "the empty has replaced the full"—an ultra-sophisticated version of the modernist slogan "less is more." Inside these dramatic spaces, the framework of the decor is graphic and very composed; often black and white, it highlights the least movement of an article of clothing, whose colors and textures are amplified by the intensity of halogen light.

Small theaters of the street, these showrooms are the image of the Kabuki or No theater, in which one admires the precision of gestures and the beauty of clothes in a minimalist setting.

When discussing the art of packaging in Japan, Roland Barthes could well have been describing the showrooms of today, "The box acts as sign: as envelope, screen, mask, it is equal to that which it hides, protects, and at the same time designates; it creates change . . . To find the object that is in the package, the signifier that is in the sign, is to throw it away; what the Japanese bring, with a formicant

energy, are empty signs."[2] Other showrooms, on a different scale, reflect the urban landscape of the 1980's. Huge spaces on two or three levels, they take on American dimensions. The most striking examples of this are the Esprit showrooms in Europe and Creeks in France. Between a small boutique and a department store, they present diverse products in enormous interiors, yet everything shares a common system of cultural reference. Their ambiance, closer to the stages of cinema than theater, reflects the imagery of Hollywood or amusement parks to capture the attention of their visitors. Fascinated by the lights, the music, the arrangement of certain furniture or pieces of architecture, visitors love to walk around as much as buy. From staircases to framework, everything supports the scenography.

Some of these places go beyond the simple idea of shop, presaging perhaps the year 2000. They offer other services closer to leisure activities: a cafe, a restaurant/bar, electronic games, videos, rest spaces, and so on, integrated into the sales space. In other words, the services offered identify fashion and life styles.

Ephemeral architecture
Whatever their dimensions, these new showrooms occupy an important position in architectural creation, becoming a sufficient pretext for well-known architects to express their talent. Free from the constraints of large-scale buildings, they realize stage sets of illusion, of dreams, of futility, of banality, of the extraordinary, of the chic, of the vulgar, of old, of young, of empty, of full, of nothing . . . But, paradoxically, this so-called ephemeral architecture rivals, in its treatment of details and its use of new technologies and luxurious materials (marble, granite, wood, steel, granito), so-called permanent architecture. From these contradictions, mixed with the needs of marketing, is born an increasing interest in these spaces. It brings new meaning to the question Robert Venturi posed in Learning from Las Vegas: "Why is there no hierarchy of architectural forms?"[3] A certain reticence nonetheless exists among a number of architects who consider commercial spaces (as opposed to houses or public buildings) outside the realm of architecture. Even if commerce

With the 1980's, a flowering of high design boutiques appeared in the four corners of the world, signaling the changes of our age.

1. Italo Calvino, Les villes invisibles, Les villes et les signes 1, Editions du Seuil, 1974.

2. Roland Barthes, L'empire des signes, Skira-Le sentier de la créaton, Collection Champs, Flammarion, 1970.

is one of the oldest of human and urban activities, it is not so much a prohibited subject, as a subject without importance. If showrooms are not among the great themes of architecture, it is not only because they present insignificant construction problems, but also because the act of consuming has more to do with imagination and fantasy than reality.

Interior design

However, can the question of showrooms still be posed as a question of architecture or nonarchitecture? That is, have the designs become more immaterial—and therefore, for some, more frivolous—by creating environments allied with fashion and the dreams and signs of a certain time? It is important that showrooms change often; in fact, their decor is fugacious and fragile, and rare are those that survive transformation. As Claude Eveno has written, they represent "the search for a tonality of the times, a search for a lifestyle of today; a trip through the interior forms of the city. Architecture closest to the body, to the pitch of its adornment. Changing spaces, to the wishes of the agreements of the intimate and the outside, of clothes and theater. The color of the 1980's."[4]

In reality, it is a question of showing how, over the last ten years, "interior design" has become sufficiently expressive that one now respects its places, its objects, and its creators. As demonstrated by the works in this book, it seems that their architecture belongs to an international language tied to fashion and to the consumption of images of modernity, constantly renewed and enriched by the arrival of the latest technology. The quality and the variety of the showrooms can be evaluated from the point of view of the spaces as well as the personalities of the men and women who created them. It is often because they are named Ettore Sottsass, Shiro Kuramata, Hans Hollein, or Philippe Starck that these places are remarkable and remarked upon, indistinguishable from a line of thought, a line of work. But a successful showroom also results from the complicity between a masterpiece and a master worker, and from the capacity of the latter to imagine spaces, from the wisest to the craziest.

International "zapping"

Although a multitude of showrooms disappear, rapidly forgotten, others become great classics, fixing on "the incredibly intense scenes of fashion and the times."[5] These unite the history of a period, the virtuosity of their creator, and the latter's capacity for innovation in the same place. The showroom of Carlo Scarpa in Venice, Loos's for Knise in Vienna, that of Mallet-Stevens for Bailly in Paris, and even those of Ruhlman and Patou for Nicolas, have become points of reference for modern showrooms. Often cited in the last fifteen years are the showrooms Shullin I and II and the travel agency in Vienna of Hans Hollein, Vittorio Gregotti's showroom for Missoni in Milan, Tadao Ando's for Step in Japan, Norman Foster's for Joseph in London, and more recently that of Kawasaki for Comme des garçons in New York. Will the stores of Ettore Sottsass in Germany or those of Joe D'Urso in the United States for Espirt, those of Starck for Creek in Paris become in their time reference points? The diversity of expression is encouraging and praiseworthy. It seems therefore difficult to report here on all the current stylistic trends; one can nonetheless contrast the moderns (or classicists) with today's baroques. In effect, yesterday's iconoclasts of modernism have become today's worshippers of modernism, through images successively sanctified from the 1930's—from high-tech, from minimalism, or from brutalism. Whereas the baroques, the neos in everything (primitives, barbarians, punks, antiquarians . . .), new iconoclasts, steal historic references and "sacred images" from modern architecture to distort them, not without kitsch, humor, and irony. Andrea Branzi writes in an Italian newspaper, "Our cultural model is no longer the pyramid, but a chessboard of tastes and styles produced by a televised society that is continually changing channels."[6]

From there, the choice of showrooms in this book can be seen as a sort of international "zapping" that does not pretend to be exhaustive. The intention has been to present projects by architects and designers both well-known and those on their way to becoming known. To show such a collection of spaces testifies to an abundance of ideas and buildings of quality, perhaps destined to be seen one day as the true style of the 1980's.

BRIGITTE FITOUSSI

3. Robert Venturi, L'Enseignement de Las Vegas, Pierre Mardaga editor, 1974.

4. Claude Evano, forward to the text "Magasinages" from Cahiers du CCI, no. 3, "Monuments éphémères" (cf. bibliography).

5. Andrée Putman, about shop windows in Le style des anées 80 (cf. bibliography).

6. Andrea Branzi, L'Espresso (weekly Italian publication), September 20, 1987.

Issey Miyake Men (cf. Visual Overview).

SCENOGRAPHY, TRADEMARK, AND INTERIOR DESIGN: NEW SALES STRATEGIES

Interview with Antonio Citterio

This thirty-eight year-old architect from Milan is responsible for a large number of interiors, the majority of which are showrooms (Mirabello, B&B, Fausto Santini, Esprit, etc.). He is also known in Italy as one of the most promising furniture designers of his generation.

Brigitte Fitoussi: You have been given many commissions for showrooms both in Italy and elsewhere. How do you conceive of these types of spaces?

Antonio Citterio: The showroom is, in my opinion, a scenographic space that is not fixed, but will change. It is equally an image, as interesting as it might be, which achieves itself irreversibly. From these givens, everything else follows. I used this discourse, which represents ten years of work, in the last Esprit store in Amsterdam, built in 1987. It was conceived as a theater, and developed for the presentation of the merchandise. This, in fact, has always been the underlying idea of my projects, along with a precise definition of the space.

What was your departure point in the Santini showrooms? Did you try to treat the spaces differently?

I spent a lot of time on the showroom projects for Fausto Santini which, in the beginning, had an associated line under the name Santini and Dominici. When they

dissolved their association, Santini found me through a little competition that included Andrea Branzi and Aldo Rossi. I was chosen and I profited from the occasion to work a great deal on the idea of the product. I thought right away that the real protagonist of the store was the shoe, and the space that held it should be a box stripped to the minimum. Several years ago, one was generally able to see all the shoe boxes in this type of store. I, on the other hand, preferred to put all the boxes in a backroom and to show only certain models on the racks. The shoe immediately became a quality product, presented in a very graphic manner.

My work is often based on very careful research of trademarks. At Santini, it was necessary to create a certain type of image and then incorporate it in future showrooms. The Santini showroom in Miami is different from that in Florence because there were two different urban contexts, two different processes. In visiting them, one understands that they are part of the same chain; they both use the same materials and the same clarity of space. But, from one place to another, the scenario is transformed. I must each time carefully reflect on the situation in which I find myself so that each showroom is designed appropriately.

Today, management seems very concerned about the problems of creating a strong identity for their companies. Do you think one can think of architecture in terms of products and merchandise, in the same way one thinks in terms of spaces and volumes?

The strategy of business is undergoing a change at this time. The tastes of people are considerably higher, as are their requirements. It is difficult to believe that they would wear a uniform, but, paradoxically, today they are much more in uniform than they were ten years ago. Only, one does not dress with just two pieces, suit and shoes, but with a whole series of coats, accessories, belts, and shoes . . . The criterium of a store of quality is that, instead of having two hundred suits to show, they have only five, six, or ten, and that's all. There is little merchandise because the idea of inventory no longer exists. Before, the department store gave us the impression of having "a hundred thousand" articles that one could buy . . .

Today, everything has changed, and one prefers products that demonstrate good taste. One trusts much more the shop that has several attractive models to one that has everything. The image of a store sells products; this is a rule. In Italy, we say, "The cloak does not make a monk, but the store makes the product."

Objectively, does one need a great deal of money to make a shop work?

It is often possible to work at a very low price, as was the case with the first showrooms for Mirabello. They had, in the beginning, superb spaces with low prices. On the other hand, my latest showrooms for Esprit cost a great deal because there was nothing there with which to start. We had to create the place, the space. It's this type of intervention that requires money.

What have been your influences? Do you have some special influences?

Like everyone, I have influences; architects who say they don't are telling stories. There is always a "before" and an "after." We always start with what we've seen, with the emotions a certain space has given us. I cannot forget the work of Carlo Scarpa, his famous showroom for Olivetti in Venice. Likewise, I cannot deny having seen the showrooms for Comme des garçons in New York, Tokyo, and Paris, as well as Kuramata's projects for Esprit. The arrival of the Japanese in the market-place has been a determinant not only for me but for other architects, because they taught us the art of showing clothes: in an empty space, a plane of wood on a plane of concrete . . . In all the cities I visit, I go see what Untel has done. These are what I would call my influences.
But well before I'd begun to work, there were also influences from well-known works. When I was a student, I watched Scarpa. My first architectural projects were completely under this influence. But, often, one looks to see what others are doing before one knows which direction to take.

Interview with Brigitte Fitoussi, in September, 1987 in Milan.

Interview with Doug Tomkins

Founder and owner of Esprit, Doug Tomkins has conquered the entire world not only as a maker of clothes and sportswear accessories, but also as distributor of his own trademark, building for himself "star spaces." Behind the withdrawn allure of this man, a smiling and active 40 year-old, one perceives an implacable "machine" whose motto is "no detail is small." This ideal is behind the architecture, design, and graphics of Esprit. Created in 1969, Esprit now has more than 100 stores, with franchises in the four corners of the world, the majority of which are in the United States, realizing revenues of 800 million dollars in 1987.

Brigitte Fitoussi: Why are large companies like yours so attentive to their showrooms today? What have become the key arguments for launching labels and products?

Doug Tomkins: That's pretty easy. I believe that, if you want to develop a coherent and perceptible image, you need to create a sensibility around the product, because you are not just selling a physical product . . . To sell a product with sensibility, there are several rules: pay attention to the wrappings, packagings, to advertising, graphic images, the sales ambience, and, of course, the presentation of the articles on the shelves, in the windows . . . It's a whole chain of elements, which if broken by a weak or

missing element, could ruin the general ambiance.

And architecture?

It's a whole. Architecture creates in some sense the ambiance in accord with the products and all the elements I mentioned. It organizes forms, colors . . . It is absolutely essential not to fail, because a showroom costs a lot of money. One cannot change it every year, especially if the architecture is monumental. It's necessary to foresee everything upstream in the project. In my opinion, shopping is either agreeable or not as a function of the showroom.

Why do you choose different architects each time to create your spaces?

I generally choose different architects because we are in different countries, in different regions. Beyond the architecture, the presentation of the merchandise—what we call "display"—is fundamental. In all our stores, there are common traits: the way mannequins are dressed, their position in the window . . . There is an image more or less identical, a common thread recognizable in all the showrooms: our logo, the products, the photos, the advertisments . . . The choice of different architects is justified by a need for perfection. I want architectural quality of the first order, which is impossible to find in one architect. The mass production of a design would diminish it. Benetton, for

example, which has multiplied the same type of store on an international scale, rapidly depreciated its initial image after the first ten showrooms.

As a general rule, what is the philosophy of Espirt, from both the point of view of the product as well as sales?

Our clothes are designed for a rather young clientele. If the consumer, the client, wears a lifestyle, we think that each of our employees should have the same line of thought as the client. That is, the employee is also a consumer, a client. At Esprit, we represent in this sense a lifestyle . . . This is why all of our young employees who want to are also part of our market; they understand how to live in the ambiance of our label, of our fashion. Perhaps it is easier for them to work here because they identify with their place of work, with Esprit. Each morning, when they arrive, they are certainly happier than those who work in a company whose products do not please them. This cycle works well because it is as positive for the employees as for our clients. Finally, the company sells products because it is "circular" and charged with the energy of the individual. This is true synergy.

Interview with Brigitte Fitoussi in September, 1987 in Milan, at the first Esprit offices in Italy.

ANTONIO CITTERIO

FAUSTO SANTINI
FLORENCE   1983

An architect by training, Antonio Citterio moves with great ease in the world of interior design and decoration. He leaves behind him not only a long list of built architectural interiors, but also furniture manufactured by the most noted producers of contemporary Italian furniture (including B&B, Boffi, and Flexform). His approach to architecture is simple, always strictly faithful to a modern treatment of object and space. His poetics of space can be summed up as follows: rigor, minimalism, and perfectionism, tied to an almost obsessive attention to detail. In 1983, an important Italian manufacturer of shoes, Fausto Santini, trusted Citterio with their image, and asked him to design their different showrooms around the world.

Shown here is one of his designs, situated in one of the pedestrian shopping streets in Florence. It is found in a medieval building. Except for the sign, the architect did not change the facade, which was to be preserved. His design was exclusively interior (the space was originally a shop). The window is pulled slightly back from the street. Demolition affected only later additions to the original building; the original walls were not touched. Santini eliminated an existing staircase and completely emptied the space. The project uses a classic language: perspective, symmetry, black, and white. The facade of the window, like the plan of the store, is organized along a central symmetrical axis. The stair was built behind partitions in the back; it rises directly

to a small mezzanine. At this level, one circulates around a narrow metallic passageway that circumscribes the entire perimeter of the store. From the ground floor, the ancient ceiling and vaults are visible through this technological structure, but it preserves its integrity due to the transparency of the system. The spare furniture picks up the colors and materials of the showroom and compliments the decor. In this purist ambiance of black and white, one can better perceive the spots of color and the models on display, which become the strong elements of the scenography. "The central idea that emerges from the design of this series of showrooms," says Citterio, "is the creation of a sort of void created from the abstraction of the scenario."

Client: *Fausto Santini, Rome.*
Products: *Shoes.*
Location: *via Calzaiuoli 95, Florence.*
Architect: *Antonio Citterio.*
Collaborators: *V. Casiraghi, G. Trabattoni, M. Veronesi, C. Theill.*
Date of completion: *1983.*
Materials: *Pure white marble for the floor, panels of white opaline for the walls, ceilings finished according to an ancient Florentine procedure resembling Venetian stucco, central seat in bands of black and white marble with feet of steel and chrome, halogen lights, sconces and fixtures (prototypes) designed by Antonio Citterio and Piero Castiglioni.*
Floor Area: *62.5 square meters: 52 on the ground floor, 10.5 above.*

The narrow metal passageway on the second floor circumscribes a large central void, allowing the main space below to be a double-height space. The general composition, very geometric, is punctuated by horizontal planes and vertical lines that are superimposed in a game of transparency and differing thicknesses. The opalescent lighting of the walls is characteristic of the material used, white opaline, which softens the contrasts of the boutique. Above the central space, six lights are aligned on axis. The cast iron fixtures are suspended by rigid poles six meters long and contain small halogen bulbs.

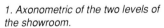

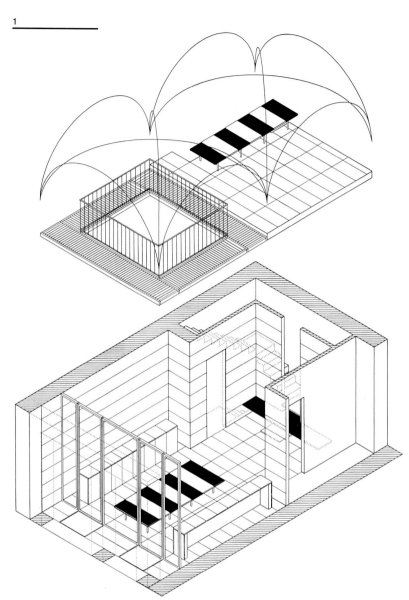

1. Axonometric of the two levels of the showroom.

2. The small mezzanine of the upper level is built of marble and opaline. It sits beneath a roof of groin vaults, an authentic medieval structure restored by using original techniques with a coating of Tuscan stucco. The rediscovery of this ancient technique, related to Venetian marmorino, allows the suggestion of aging by mimicking the cracks and imperfections that characterize walls in historic places. The hardware that attaches the lamps to the ceiling recalls the conical form of the reflectors.

3. View from above: symmetrical composition of the countertops on each side of the central seating.

4. Project sketch.
5. The central plane of black and white marble serves both as seating and as a countertop. "This furnished void," Citterio's principal intention for the project, gives the Santini showroom a very graphic quality.
6. Sketch of the site in Florence.
7. Facade of the showroom. The window is slightly pulled back from the street to create an independent reading of the interior architecture from the exterior.

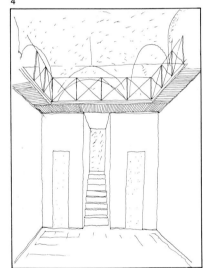

M. BARDELLI
MILAN 1986

Situated in an old Milanese building and conceived as a large closet, the last showroom realized by Studio Gregotti takes a small part of the city as its scheme. There are no windows on the facade. There is only a foyer that opens onto the collection of Bardelli clothing, the reputation of which is well-established in Italy. The architects were presented with an unusual site, from the point of view of the introduction of typology. From a long passageway, perhaps an ancient passage for carts, one comes upon a sort of irregular niche, articulated on several barely discernible levels. This was undoubtedly an ancient courtyard, excavated to gain access to the basement, then covered by subsequent renovations.

The theme of the project was to order this articulated and richly layered space to create a showroom for sophisticated clothes and accessories, and to perpetuate a tradition in the style of presenting merchandise. The street facade was cleaned and restored, and the traditional metal sign, often used in this area, was kept. The old passageway was transformed into an interior street along which the windows are organized: it terminates in the reception and payment area that serve the two floors of the store. The first level, lower down, is characterized by a polygon of shelves that is followed by a narrow circular mezzanine, accessible by a staircase hidden in the thickness of the walls. The result is a centralized space of two stories, a sort of cylinder made of pear wood fit in between the walls and slabs of sandstone. This rational arrangement is not encumbered by superfluous elements; only the air conditioning outlets that are arranged on the false ceiling are decorative. With a certain refinement, the architects have recharged a space that at first seemed resistant to all geometry.

Client: *M. Bardelli.*
Products: *Clothing and accessories.*
Location: *via Madonnina 19, Milan.*
Architects: *Gregotti Associates: A. Cagnardi, P.L. Cerri, V. Gregotti.*
Collaborators: *R. Pitton, P. Ferrari.*
Date of completion: *1986.*
Materials: *Gray granite, lightly polished on the floor and rough on the walls, cylinder and furniture in pink pear wood, display windows with metal mullions painted green, interior in cashmere, low wattage halogen lights remotely controlled, directional spot lights recessed in false ceilings and cases.*
Floor area: *170 square meters total (gallery and mezzanine); 120 on the ground floor, 50 on the mezzanine.*

View of the principle interior level. For each type of clothing, the architects have designed a specific type of display for a very rational presentation. The shelves, reveal, banister, and ceiling are all of pear wood. The floor is laid with panels of gray granite.

1

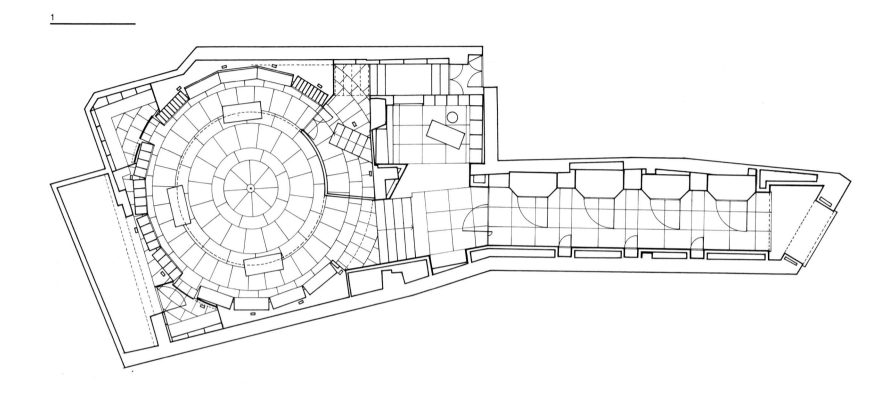

2

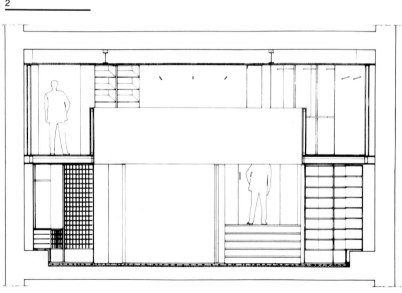

3

1. Plan.
2. Transverse section.
3. Entry to the store from the interior street along which display windows are aligned.
4. Access lower down to the central circular space, after several steps.

5. Interior of the principal cylindrical volume, seen from the entry.
6. Cashier's desk, treated as a small intimate office with its own library. Space tucked in between the mezzanine above and the cylindrical voume below.
7. Access to the mezzanine.

4

5

6

7

CLAUDIO NARDI

LUISA VIA ROMA
FLORENCE   1984

The Luisa showroom is found in a nineteenth-century building in the center of Florence. The architect preserved only the landmarked facade (columns and arcades) as an element in his design: a sort of folding screen from the previous century that plays a unifying role between the new and old typologies of the city. Behind the proscenium, he has created a new "urban theater," parallel but distant, separated by a play of shadows.

Using the imagery of a game of Chinese boxes, he suggests a new city, only just built, which, instead of being completely hidden by its ancient shell (sole survivor after the demolition), is instead revealed by it. Inside the showroom, a sales gallery conceived as a sort of covered market proposes a continuous urban itinerary: a street, its outlets, natural light. Working on two levels, Luisa has not been designed as a department store, but as if it were made up of several shops found in the same place; the products themselves are very diversified. Every-

thing has been realized in natural materials and colors: white walls, unfinished wood, and marble.

The architect recovered a beautiful source of natural light by building a large skylight, situated in the middle of the store. The skylight hovers above a terrace used as an open space for music, theater, visual arts, and, of course, fashion receptions.

This restoration, born in the l'air du temps, hopes to be outside time, yet, in the end, reflects its own time.

Client: *Andrea Paconesi.*
Products: *Clothing, shoes, men's and women's accessories.*
Location: *via Roma 21, Florence.*
Architect: *Claudio Nardi.*
Collaborator: *Maurizio de Marco.*
Date of completion: *1984.*
Materials: *Pavement in parquet and marble with a decorative motif. White shelves in wood and brazilian quartz. Structure and clothes racks in black iron, staircase in natural wood. Windows in iron, with glass and opaline.*
Floor area: *500 square meters.*
Cost: *Approximately 600,000 dollars.*

Perspective from the ground floor in the principle space, conceived as a covered gallery with artificially-lit arcades on either side. The enormous skylight, composed of rectangular metal frames painted in white, covers the length of the entire central space, filling it with daylight. The check-out desk, situated on the entry axis, is situated at the back of the store and serves as a guard desk to the stairs that lead to the terrace. The floor has been covered with parquet and varnished matte.

1. A second plane, behind the arcades of the preserved historic facade, is the true exterior facade of the store.
2. Under the arcades, inside the covered gallery, treatment of a niche in trompe-l'oeil; on the wall at the back of the niche, a painted scene and a wash of pastel colors, from sky-blue to water-green.
3. The terrace, accessible from the interior of the store, seen across the large parallel-piped skylight.
4. Detail of the glass banister of the circular staircase leading to the basement
5. This spiral staircase, which leads to the shoe department, unfolds in the space with a generous curve due to the very slight rise of the steps.
6. Axonometric.
7. Plans of the first and second levels.

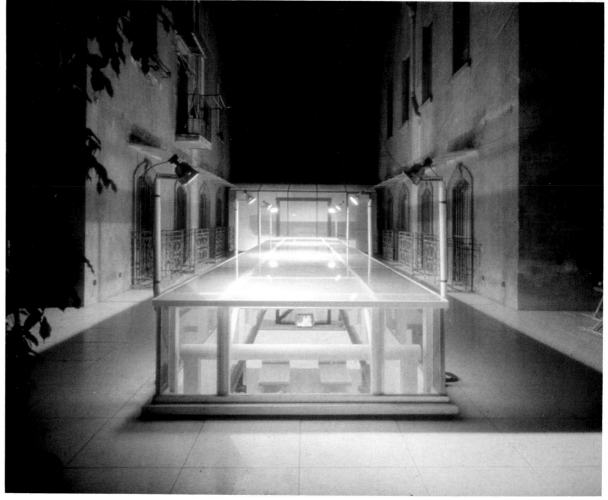

4

5

6

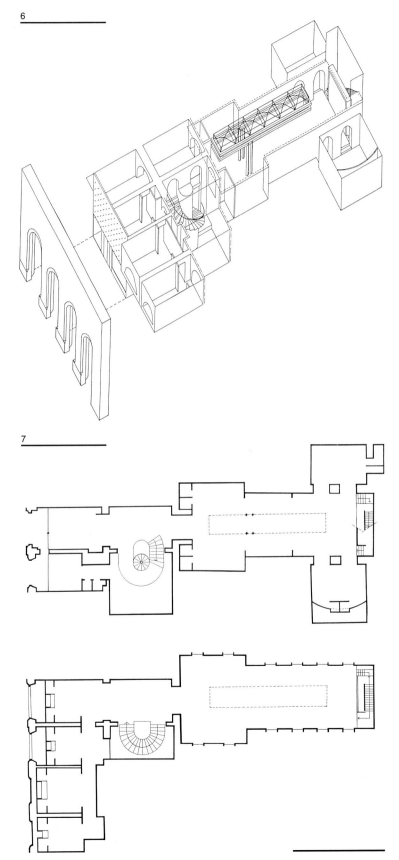

7

CLINO TRINI CASTELLI
ACHILLE CASTIGILIONI

CASSINA

MILAN 1985–1987

A high spot in Italian design, the Cassina showroom is well known to visitors of the Milan Furniture Show who come here each fall. An obligatory stop for amateur admirers of novelties, the showroom has become a place of conviviality and cosmopolitan exchange, of movement and creativity. From the simple stroller to the most prestigious designer, everyone wanders, admires, criticizes, or tests the famous *divanis* installed under the central dome of the boutique.

It is necessary to note that Cassina has become well-known both by recreating the works of the masters of modernism and by producing works of the avant-garde. This small company, whose beginnings were more artisanal than industrial, was founded at the end of the last century to produce wooden furniture. Today, the company is one of the leading manufacturers of high design furniture.

The Milanese showroom has become symbolic of this continuous research by presenting itself, over the years, not only as an exhibition space but also as a background to various displays. Following successive designs by Mario Bellini and Vico Magistretti, it fell to Clino Trini Castelli to transform the space. He created a "pavilion of gray light" in the large central space under a metallic cupola supported on asymmetrically arranged poles—the largest reflector of "gray light" ever built. It acts like the back of a cat's eye by reflecting back to its source every luminous ray that strikes it. It is a cold but beautiful light which, according to Castelli, belongs in "a conceptual fashion to the penumbra." Built in 1985, this project created a surreal atmosphere but did not address adequately the lighting problems that an exhibition space of this size presents. Therefore, in 1987, Achille Castiglioni made subsequent renovations. He created a system of adjustable lighting with pendants suspended from thin metal rods. These rods striate the space in height, but disappear when fully lit by casting on the ceiling an immense web of luminous points. This perfect simplicity, which preserves and augments the intention of the original project, reminds us that light can clearly define a space. And also that Castiglioni rightly deserves his reputation as a grand designer.

Client: *Cassina, Milan.*
Products: *Contemporary furniture.*
Location: *via Durini, Milan.*
Architects: *CDM Castelli Design: Clino Trini Castelli and Marek N. Piotrovski (interiors), Elena Lorena, Claudia Raimondo (window display), Antonio Petrillo (lighting).*
Date of completion: *1985 (renovation of existing showroom).*
Floor area: *983 square meters (including offices that open onto the showroom).*

Architect: *Achille Castiglioni.*
Date of completion: *1987 (renovation of Castelli project).*
Lighting: *The canopies have diffusers in the shape of a truncated cone, in frosted plexiglass, with a transparent center.*

1. View from under the arcades toward the reflective metal cupola, built in 1985 for Cassina by Clino Trini Castelli. "The pavilion of gray light" reflects all rays of light that hit it towards its center and creates, according to the varying intensity of the light fixtures and ambiant light, unique coloration. It is the largest light reflector ever built. On the ground, the power cords are encrusted in the floor, and, along with the floor are painted over in a gray parquet varnish.
2. Detail of the metallic cupola with its neoclassical design.
3. Section through the cupola.
4. Plan of the showroom.

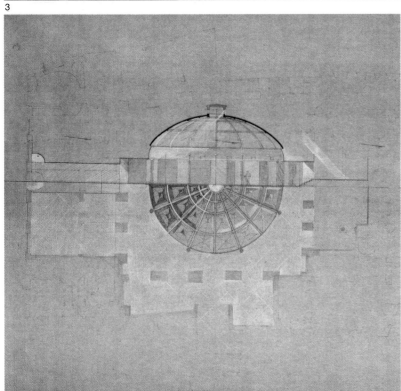

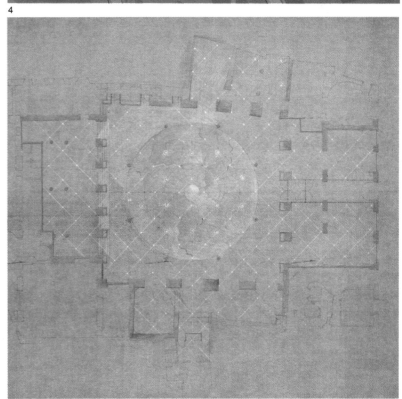

1

2

1. General view of the central space of the Cassina showroom under the metal cupola, designed by Clino Trini Castelli.
2. New showroom built by Achille Castiglioni in 1987. This project modified the existing lighting and rationalized the interior spaces. The floor was completely redone and the heavy columns were replaced by slender steel poles. A series of modular partitions mounted on wheels articulates the large central space. The metal cupola was conserved but the lighting was radically transformed by a system of canopies that give the space a lively intense luminosity.
3. Detail of suspended canopies with diffusers in the form of a truncated cone of frosted plexiglass. The thin metal bars that support the fixtures disappear when everything is illuminated.

3

ESPRIT
COLOGNE   1986

Doug Tomkins, founder and president of Esprit,[1] decided to transform the image of his company in the early 1980's. He created "star spaces" around the world by using the biggest names in design and architecture.

Fascinated by the quality and originality of the work of Ettore Sottsass and his associates—from the Fiorucci boutiques to the resounding and unforgettable creations of Memphis—Doug Tomkins chose them to design the gigantic showrooms in West Germany (Hamburg, Dusseldorf, Berlin, Cologne). The Cologne store is clearly inspired by the forms and materials of Memphis. The walls seem in effect to tell the history of this explosive Italian firm, "The unfurling of the baroque and the uncertain, of color and insanity, of the gadget and the sale, of invention and the wink, of recollection and adaptation, of humor and the frankly comic," as Gilles de Bure wrote in his last book.[2]

The sales space unfolds on three levels. The entrance, situated on the intermediate floor, passes above on a suspended passageway. The lower level is embellished by a mezzanine inaccessible to the public, which houses offices and services (bathrooms, kitchen, snack bar, computer and video rooms). The three levels are connected by a sculptural staircase, characterized by a complex articulation of volumes. It opens up in a series of pink forms, which are sensual and monochromatic, in opposition to the surfaces of the walls and floor, which are more uniform and entirely covered in pointillist ceramics.

The organization of the space is not very complicated. Strongly personal elements make up the composition. The scale is constantly interrupted by giant furnishings, which become architecture, and by the bright colors, which become furniture. Esprit is thus transformed into an immense amusement park of clothing. Where does design stop and architecture begin? The Cologne store is a representative example of the emergence of interior design in the 1980's.

1. See interview, p. 8.
2. Gilles de Bure, Ettore Sottsass, (Paris: Rivages, 1987).

Client: *Esprit de Corp, Cologne.*
Products: *Clothing, accessories, men's and women's sportswear.*
Location: *Hohe strasse 160–168, Cologne, West Germany.*
Architects: *Sottsass Associates: Ettore Sottsass and Aldo Cibi, with Shuji Hisada.*
Associate architects: *Lindener and Partners (Cologne), Karl Switze (Esprit de Corp).*
Lighting consultant: *Hans von Malotki with Licht Design.*
Materials: *Wall and floor coverings in multicolor Granito; stair railings plastered with pink marmorino (Italian specialty made of marble powder); handrails in black metal; elevator in transparent glass with painted metal structure; shelves and counters in color laminates and pressboard; conference room table in laminate with printed motifs designed by Sottsass.*
Floor area: *1000 square meters on three levels.*
Cost: *Approximately 3,000,000 dollars.*

View from the top level of the Esprit store, showing two levels below (the total area is imposing: more than 1,000 square meters). This angular structure is situated above the main entrance to the store, which is on the ground floor. From the street, the visitor crosses a passageway suspended above the void of the basement. All the general spaces are made up of this overlapping of stacked and asymmetrical volumes, which are covered in bright colors and materials dear to Memphis: printed laminates, granito, and terrazzo.

1. View of the elevator shafts of transparent glass, with metal structure and doors of gray and white marble.
2. Detail of the furnishings. Shelves and racks with integrated mirrors: a modular element built of pastel-colored laminate.
3. Variation of the furnishings with different functional composition: here, a rack with two different levels for hanging clothes.
4. Detail of the stair and its sculptural volumes. Ceramics on the floor and walls in granito.
5. The walls of the staircase are realized in pink marmorino, a specially treated marble powder. Embedded lights follow the steps. The handrails in black-painted metal are bent to achieve a sense of movement.

1

2

  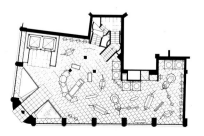

3

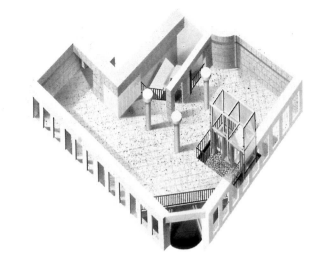

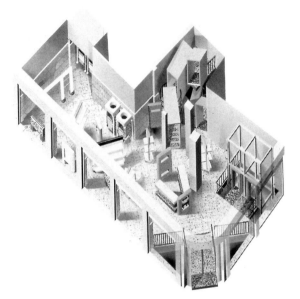

1. Cashier's counter, very similar to Memphis's formal vocabulary. It is made of a juxtaposition of diverse plastic laminate elements of all forms and colors (blue, red, green, pink, and yellow) combined with spots of black and white and with reconstituted chestnut-grained wood.

2. Floor plans: basement, street level, and second floor.
3. Axonometric sketches of the three floors. The basement also has a small mezzanine housing offices and services.
4. Dressing rooms.
5. Detail of the multicolored cashier's desk engraved with the Esprit logo.

EDUARD SAMSO

TERESA RAMALLAL
BARCELONA 1986

The young Catalan architect Eduard Samso has to his credit more than fifteen built architectural interiors located, for the most part, in Barcelona. These projects have propelled him to the forefront of Spanish design.

The Ramallal boutique, like most of Samso's projects, manifests a minimalist sensibility. Samso seeks here a purification of line and a maximum reduction of designed form. Inspired by a revival of the notion of "less is more," he replaces crowded spaces with emptiness. His interiors are extremely simple in appearance because he uses few elements; here he punctuates the space with several stainless-steel columns and curved sheets of transparent glass. All of the furnishings were designed down to the smallest details, providing a subtle backdrop for the shoes in the window.

1

Client: *Teresa Ramallal, fashion designer, Barcelona.*
Products: *Women's clothing and shoes.*
Location: *Maestro Nicolau, 17, Barcelona.*
Architect: *Eduard Samso.*
Date of completion: *1986.*
Floor area: *Approximately 60 square meters.*

1. View of interior. All furnishings were designed by Eduard Samso and constructed of frosted glass and tubes of chrome-plated steel.
2. View of the front window from outside, at night. The window is made of glass panels that expose the interior. The front door is made of chrome-plated metal. The marquee alters the scale of the shop on the street front by dividing the great height of the interior volume. The minimalist space is counterbalanced by a series of simple details, such as the shoe stands in the front window, which are raised on metal stems and which give the impression that the shoe models are suspended in the void.

**TONET SUNYER
TOMAS MORATO**

JOACHIM BERRAO

BARCELONA 1984

This small jewelry store was conceived in the image of Berrao's jewelry: elegant without being precious, sober without being insipid, as stylish as it is rigorous. The architects' first built work, the shop reveals a mastery of space and materials. The arrangement is minimal, but the architects have made clever use of transparencies, grooves, and movable partitions to give the effect of a "magic chest." The project acquires its strength from the ease with which the transition from exterior to interior was realized. Because the shop was very small and elongated, it was designed according to functionalism, then enhanced by small touches that yield beautiful visual effects. The lighting counts as much as the display cases; it intensifies the interior ambiance by contrasting cold, diffused ceiling lights with the more direct ones over the display cases. The removable cases are mounted on the wall by means of a system of metal rails that allows them to be slid along the wall. The graphic effect of the boutique is reinforced by the black lines of the metalwork, the vertical cords of the lights, and the hollow grooves appearing along the baseboards, railings, and steps. Note the references to Scarpa and MacIntosh. The materials used are not luxurious—glass, wood, stucco, iron, and treated concrete for the floor—but the result is nonetheless quite sophisticated.

Client: *Joachim Berrao, designer, Barcelona.*
Products: *Designer jewelry.*
Location: *calle Rosellon, 227, Barcelona.*
Architects: *Tonet Sunyer and Tomas Morato.*
Builder: *Construcciones Royo.*
Date of completion: *December 1984.*
Floor area: *25 square meters.*
Cost: *Approximately 750 dollars per square meter.*

View of the interior. Because of the narrowness of the space, the architects emphasized the height of the volume with a lengthwise spatial organization. On the first floor one sees small removable display cases made of thick transparent glass. They are mounted on a black-painted metal support along which they can slide from the edges of the walls to the center. The lamps, made of long metal stems with simple ferrules and bare bulbs, hang from the ceiling. Arranged symmetrically, they illuminate the display cases below, which, topped with opaque discs, send indirect light back onto the walls. The pieces of jewelry can thus be viewed without excessive glare.

TONET SUNYER
TOMAS MORATO

1. Longitudinal section.
2. Axonometric.
3. Detail of staircase.
4. Sales desk and cash register. The furniture is made of black wood with brass-plated legs. The floor is varnished concrete. The creviced baseboards accentuate the graphic quality of the boutique.
5. View of the entrance facing the front window.
6. Facade from the exterior.
7. Detail of a display case.
8. Construction detail of display case.

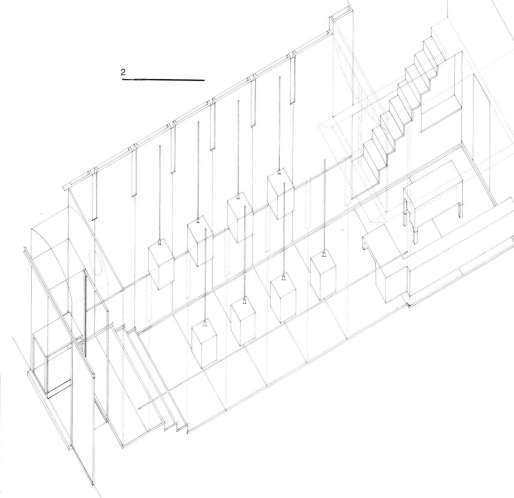

5

6

7

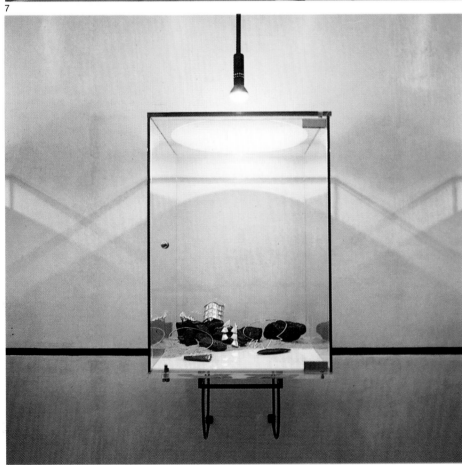

8

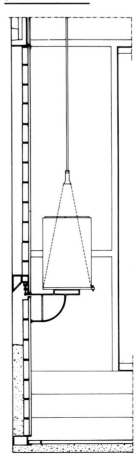

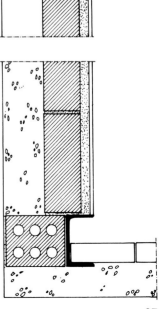

SWATCH
NANTUCKET 1987

1

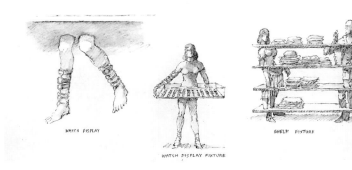

WATCH DISPLAY

WATCH DISPLAY FIXTURE

SHELF FIXTURE

The Site group continues to elaborate the provocative themes of its early projects, dating from over fifteen years ago. Site's projects are always challenging the borders between art and architecture, good and bad taste, humor and cynicism.

This new showroom for Swatch, where watches and T-shirts are sold to retailers, was built in an old warehouse difficult to reuse because of its narrow shape. The existing space had a tiny facade, given its 300 square meters of surface area, and a ceiling height of only 2.3 meters. Site turned these constraints to its advantage by creating a playful interior scenario out of a functional environment. In tune with Swatch's generally young and diversified clientele, the design and decor of the showroom suggest a fluid and active ambiance, whether empty or occupied. The architects have created an original space with a parade of wax mannequins, whole

and in fragments. The legs emerging from floor and ceiling, the truncated figures, and the gray silhouettes seem to be perpetually in motion. Their surreal aspect, amplified by large walls of mirrors,

totally transforms the space. Seen from afar, busts and legs appear to comprise intact bodies, whereas in reality these fragments are mounted above and below the display cases.

Client: Swatch (Parallel Marketing Corp.).
Products: Watches and sportswear.
Location: 20 Center Street, Nantucket, Massachusetts.
Architects-Designers: Site Projects: James Wines, Alison Sky, Josh Weinstein.
Consultant: Alan Goldin.
Window dresser: Architectural Sculpture Associates–Alan Swanson.
Date of completion: 1987.
Floor area: Approximately 300 square meters.

1. Preliminary sketch.
2. General view of store before installation of clothes and watches. Notice the low ceiling height, counterbalanced by the placement of the truncated mannequins. Integrated into the ceiling, the legs create an illusion enhanced by the gray surfaces of the space.
3. Perspective. A wall of videos is installed at the back of the store.
4. Detail of a display case in which a bust appears to be imbedded.
5. Display case for Swatch watches.

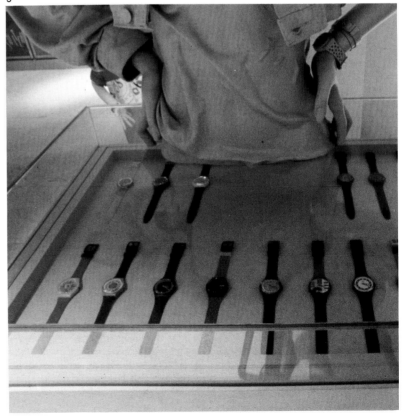

HANS HOLLEIN

SHULLIN II
VIENNA   1982

Having achieved a certain notoriety, the jeweler Herbert Shullin decided to expand his shop (its 15 square meters were no longer sufficient) in 1981. Shullin I, built by Hans Hollein in 1972, was remarkably well-conceived in its details and was famous for the originality of its facade designed in the form of a fault line. It was unthinkable not to do something equitable with the new store. Hence, despite time constraints (construction of Shullin I took over a year) and the high cost of Hollein's first project, the jeweler decided once again in favor of the virtuosity of this Viennese architect. And, in the end, Shullin II is the fruit of an exceptional effort. It resembles a luxurious jewelry box from *The Thousand and One Nights*: a curious realm where the Queen of Saba and Joseph Hoffmann exist side by side. Hollein, who seems to like indefinite and archaic historical references, mixes periods and cultures in a sort of reinvented atavism. He takes up themes from the Viennese tradition in his own fashion, emphasizing theatricality, ostentation, and sensuality. The refinement of the materials is so sophisticated that the exotic red wood of the furniture becomes confounded with Veronese marble of the same shade.

Not everything here was designed under the sign of opulence; Hollein easily mixes "rich" and "poor" materials in a way that one does not at first glance detect, as in the gold-plated industrial steel at the top of the columns or the laminated plywood imitating marble. The furniture takes exuberant shapes; conspicuously designed, it enhances the store. Both commercial space and intimate salon, the jewelry shop offers two scenarios of selling in two distinct spaces. At the entrance is the exhibition space and cash register; behind this lies a space with a round table and armchairs for reflection and transactions.

Having become a landmark in the Austrian capital, the Shullin II jewelry shop remains today a perfect model of the baroque approach to design.

Client: *Herbert Shullin, Vienna.*
Products: *Jewelry.*
Location: *Kholmark, Vienna.*
Architect: *Hans Hollein.*
Collaborators: *Wolfgang Schoefl, Manfred Bukowski, Erich Pedevilla.*
Sculptor: *Géro Schwanberg (doorknobs).*
Date of completion: *1982.*
Materials: *Wawona red wood for the furniture, Veronese marble for the floors, Stuccolustro columns topped by industrial torchères, gold-plated industrial metal.*
Floor area: *Approximately 80 square meters.*

The memorable facade of the jewelry store Shullin II, which has become a landmark. Above the boutique itself, a neon arc echoes the form of the entrance portico. The composition of the two windows is symmetrical. These are separated by the narrow doorway, which is slightly recessed to form a small entryway. The two columns of the portico are made of rough-hewn wood.

!. Exterior view of entrance.
2. Doorknob made by sculptor Géro
Schwanberg.
3. Axonometric.

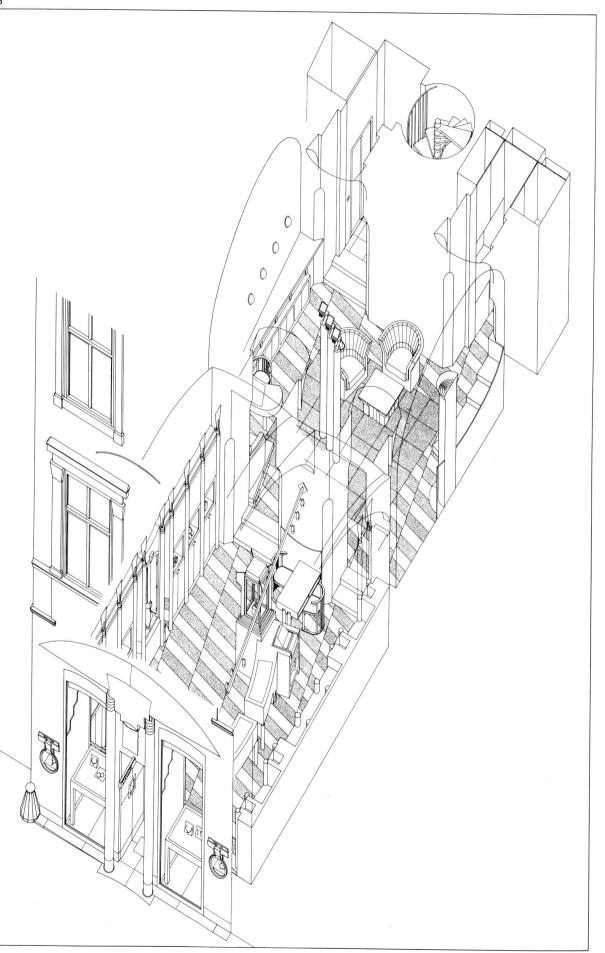

42

4. View from the entrance: the cashier's desk and exotic red wood display cases. The marble floor is patterned in bicolored stripes. The luminous columns between the display cases are topped by hammered aluminum sheeting.
5. Plan of the jewelry shop.
6. Salon space. The three lamps imbedded in the floor are made of imitation marble supports and powerful industrial torchères. The monochromatic white marble floor, unique to this space, marks a separation from the reception area.

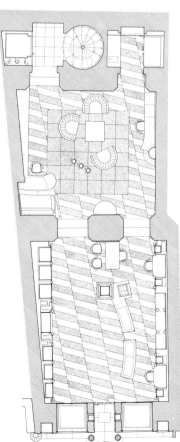

COOP HIMMELBLAU

KON'YO SHEN'TE
TOKYO   1987

Whether they are working in Vienna or in Tokyo, Coop Himmelblau constructs spaces in tension by accentuating perspectives, disrupting orthogonal elements, and designing "sharply and acutely." The architects strive to create a climate of dramatic intensity. Here, in the Nishi Azabu quarter of Tokyo, they created in a small space a gallery-boutique for artists' objects. The work sold here comes from all over the world. Their display within the gallery is organized into three categories: industrial objects, limited edition designs, and artworks or one-of-a-kind pieces. Signaled at the entrance by a sort of periscope, the boutique, half-buried, is entirely lit by its high windows. Just barely across the threshold, all is movement and oblique angles above a floor of narrow wood slats. The display furniture is highly designed: sections of glass suspended by cables and metal tubing. In the center an enormous, bright red sculpture—an irregular cone—warps the dimensions of the space.

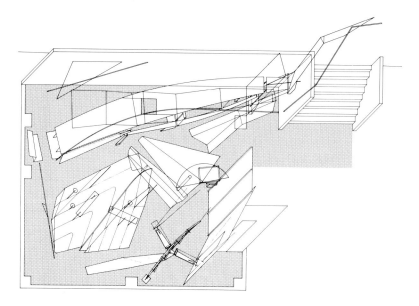

Client: *Jiva Company, Tokyo.*
Products: *Artists' objects, fashion, and art.*
Architects: *Coop Himmelblau: Wolf D. Prix and H. Swiczinski.*
Associated Architect: *(in Tokyo) Nakamura Kensetsu.*
Date of completion: *1987.*
Floor area: *100 square meters.*

Interior view of the metal footbridge, which is both sculptural and functional. It crosses the center of the gallery and rests on three supports. A single, slender metal column is visible; the others are hidden in the walls. The loads are transferred to the side walls by means of an intermediary structural system.

BAUMANN STUDIO-GALLERY
VIENNA 1985

Eric Baumann, graphic designer and collector, wanted a studio in which he could work and also display his friends' artworks. His requirements stopped there, but his choice of architects was not insignificant. With Prix and Swiczinski, the two accomplices of Coop Himmelblau, he was assured of obtaining an architecture that he could exhibit on the same level as his friends' work. The Viennese firm has a habit of creating spaces with construction systems as complex as they are ethereal.

In this case the challenge was to redesign a small space (a room of 50 square meters, 5 meters in height, with a triple-arched arcade along the facade) in a valuable piece of Viennese real estate. The architects envisioned high walls and doorways, removable staircases, light platforms, bridges, and galleries. They also conceived of three bands of pictures along the back wall: two visible from the floor and a third perceivable from a footbridge. The original surface area was increased by 20 square meters with the addition of a small platform.

On the facade, two of the archways serve as the entranceway. One of these provides access to a raised platform by means of a galvanized steel staircase that can be lowered directly onto the sidewalk. The third archway is run through by a freestanding aluminum sculpture in the form of wings projecting out over the pavement. This three-dimensional element participates as much outside as inside in controlling light and air.

The footbridge rests on three vertical supports—slender metal columns only one of which is visible, the other two being hidden in the walls. Their loads are transferred to the side walls by an intermediary structural system. The footbridge crosses the center of the space 2.5 meters from the ceiling, leaving the 5 meters of wall space below free for hanging pictures. The bridge thus divides the space while making maximum use of it.

Client: *Eric Baumann, graphic designer, Vienna.*
Location: *Vienna 1, Borseplatz 3.*
Architects: *Coop Himmelblau: Wolf D. Prix and H. Swiczinski, with F. Mascher.*
Statics: *Oskar Graf, Vienna.*
Construction: *Metallbau Treiber, Graz.*
Date of completion: *June 1985.*
Floor area: *71 square meters.*

Interior view of display piece. Its curved form evokes movement and tension. It consists of a flat plane suspended by curved metal tubes and nautical cables. Partially underground, the gallery is lit by a longitudinal skylight.

1. Axonometric.
2. Section of the footbridge.
3. View of the ground floor facing the corner desk. The double-height ceiling (5 meters), leaves the entire wall surface free so that three rows of pictures can be hung. The top row is visible only from the footbridge.
4. Detail of the footbridge. The galvanized steel staircase, which can reach down to the sidewalk outside, is raised here.
5. Detail of the facade showing the wing-shaped aluminum sculpture in one of its three arches.
6. Facade of the studio-gallery.

1 ─────────

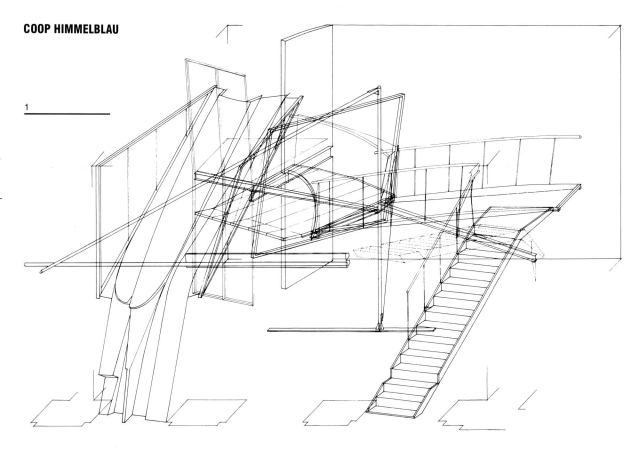

2 ─────────

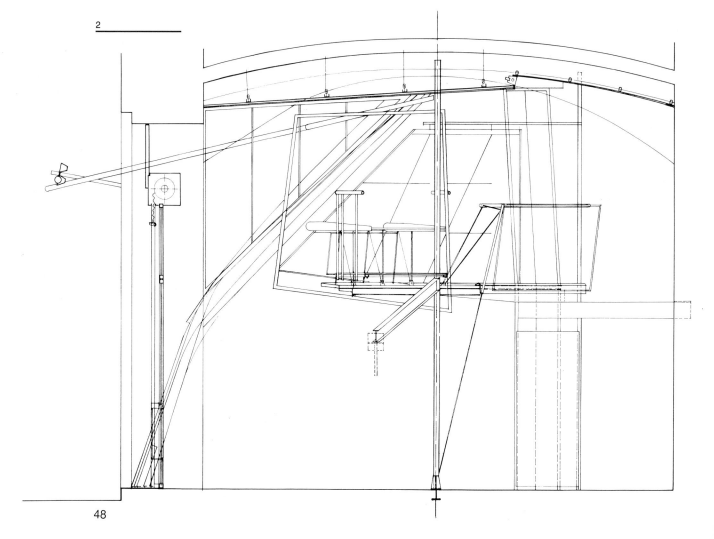

3

4

5

6

**ANDRÉE PUTMAN
ÉCART**

EBEL

LONDON   1987

In search of a new image for his boutiques, the watchmaker Ebel launched a competition for ideas in 1985. While his world is always in step with tradition, he did not escape the tyranny of the eighties look. Aware of changes in the marketplace, he hoped to respond to an international clientele that no longer associated luxury with classicism. Andrée Putman won the competition over Mario Botta and Afra and Tobia Scarpa with a project simple in appearance (because of its refinement) but elaborate in furniture and materials.

Using the theme "Architects of Time," Ebel's advertising slogan, Putman first created an exhibition stall of 300 square meters at the International Watchmaker's Fair in Basel. Here she developed the basis of a new architectural concept for Ebel's future boutiques. Its hallmark is a simple construc-tion element, the portico—the emblem of passage, an architectural archetype.

In London, on the facade of the first boutique, one finds the portico in its most simple form: two posts and a lintel, made of Portland stone, a common British finished stone. The black metal grid of the glazed parts symbolically recalls the image of the watchmaker's traditional grating. Such a modern bareness on the shop front was a first, because, in the world of high-scale watchmaking, everything is still "under gilding" and "on red velvet."

Écart also set in motion for Ebel a new commercial strategy of interior organization by designing a remarkable series of showcases and storage units. The boutique consists of an initial space for reception and display followed by a second, more intimate room for sales. Here cash registers were concealed, and sales desks were set at table height to show the client that he was dealing with specialists. Everything was studied down to the smallest details and executed without ostentation: from the display cases to the lights, from the cabinets to the baseboards to the knobs on the drawers (reeditions of Mallet-Stevens's designs).

Écart abandoned the austere black and white that made them famous for warmer and more luxurious shades, using, for example, white oak and brass. Following her interest in reeditions of thirties furniture, Andrée Putman designed furniture as sophisticated as it is sober and that, architectural itself, prevails over the architecture of the spaces. At Ebel, a new form of finery for the chic blends nonconformism with the most enduring values of tradition.

Clients: *Ebel, Switzerland.*
Products: *Watches.*
Location: *179 New Bond Street, London.*
Architects: *Écart: Andrée Putman with Thierry Conquet.*
Assistant: *Sharon MacDonald (oversaw construction in London).*
Marketing Consultant: *CMC, Jean-Bernard Maeder.*
Hardware and furniture: *Dennery.*
Date of completion: *1987.*
Materials: *Facade in Portland stone, floor in white oak, walls of off-white paint, baseboards in glass and metal, wheeled display cases in scored, pickled wood tinted with pale varnish, metalwork of brass and a combination of matte and shiny nickel, wheeled display cases with wooden trays and glass plates.*
Floor area: *80 square meters total: 60 for the sales area and 20 for office space.*

View of interior. Symmetrical arrangement of elements in the space. The main axis leads to the back of the store, to the private offices closed off by frosted glass doors. On the first floor the pickled oak furniture on wheels is composed of drawers topped by an angled glass display case. Behind is the space for transactions with its rounded sales desks. The overhead lights were specially designed for Ebel with three possible levels of illumination.

ANDRÉE PUTMAN
ÉCART

I. Plan.

2. Perspective sketch of interior volumes.

3. Working drawings of the lights over the sales desks. Movable by means of an electronic device, they are made of both matte and glossy nickel.

4. Working drawings of the wheeled display cases, made of metal and wood.

5. The sales desks were designed and made to measure. The chairs were made of pickled oak with horsehair upholstery and nickel-plated handles (on the chair backs) and legs.

6. Detail of the front window.

7. Locked cabinet, designed to hold specific merchandise, under the sales desks. These cabinets were treated as wheeled display cases with numerous drawers housing the precious merchandise.

8. Display cases. The doorknobs were designed by Mallet-Stevens and reproduced by Écart International.

9. Sketch of the facade.

1

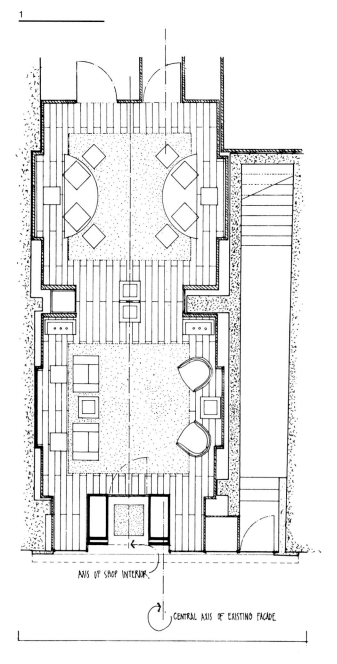

AXIS OF SHOP INTERIOR

CENTRAL AXIS OF EXISTING FACADE

2

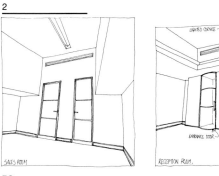

3

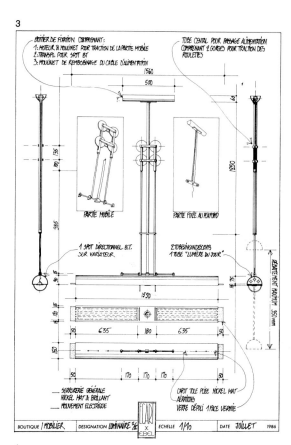

4

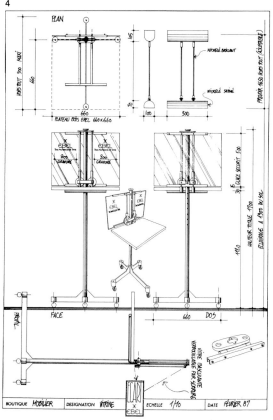

52

CREEKS
PARIS   1985

Located in the Les Halles quarter, the Creeks showroom is situated on a pedestrian street animated night and day by a series of fast-food emporia and sex shops with gaudy, catchy facades. To distinguish itself from this noisy environment, Creeks created a quiet and monumental first floor. An enormous, flat facade consists of three green marble porticos with large aluminum doors that fold back during the day and completely hide the interior after business hours. The typical notion of a shop window was abandoned. The design task was not, in the beginning, at all clear. Not only was the environment strongly defined, but the store was to be located on a plot occupied by an old building. By gutting the old structure and annexing an unused courtyard, Starck managed to create a striking space while contradicting all the familiar commercial showrooms.

His boutique has no front window and is characterized mainly by its monumental, three-story staircase. Traditionally, one would not build such a stair-case, because customers supposedly don't like having to change levels inside shops. But times have apparently changed, and a new sales scenario has evolved. Creek's mostly young clientele is fascinated by spaces with which it can identify and which allow them to dream while shopping.

Starck, much praised in recent years for his furniture and interior designs, knows precisely how to seize the changes of his day and to transcribe these changes in his projects. His talent lies in his capacity to create significant and uncommon atmospheres, to transgress the limits of taste (which he claims not to possess), to exaggerate and in so doing ennoble defects, and to enlarge and thus revalorize ordinary spaces. But he also possesses a sense of spectacle. One could well imagine an opera tenor or leather-clad rock star emerging from this gigantic, pink staircase.

At Creeks an illusion of space is created by a wall covered from top to bottom with mirrors, which reflects and hence doubles the staircase and its monumental effect. This is the realm of chrome-plated and acidic ostentation, of great, illuminated vertigo—as if the boutique's owner had wanted to compensate for the audacity of his nonexistent storefront. Even this facade, given its size, exhibits a magnificent sobriety.

Client: *Creeks, Paris.*
Products: *Clothing, accessories, men's and women's shoes, sportswear for young people.*
Location: *rue Saint-Denis, Paris.*
Architect: *Philippe Starck.*
Date of completion: *1985.*
Materials: *Facade in green marble, door panels in aluminum, staircase in pink granito, railings in chrome, wood flooring, low-voltage lights under the steps, on the floor, and in the plasterwork.*
Floor area: *400 square meters on three levels.*

View of central staircase, which is reflected in the enormous wall of mirrors to which is attached a custom-made chrome-plated clock, a trademark of several of Starck's projects. The pink steps are made of marmorino. The floor under the staircase is of light wood.

1. Facade during closing hours. It is made of dark green marble with aluminum doors.
2. Top floor. Linear wall arrangement with a series of pink cubicles.
3. View of the basement.
4. Chrome-plated railings and clothing racks.
5. Detail of volumes and cut-out forms along the staircase at the top floor.
6. Longitudinal section.

1

2

3

4

5

6

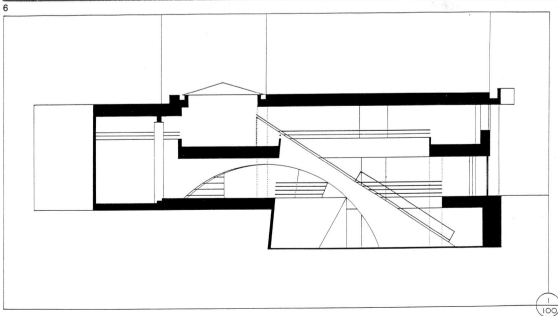

**PATRICK AND DANIEL RUBIN
CANAL**

CLAUDE MONTANA HOMMES

PARIS   1983

Soon after building Montana's first boutique for women in 1982, the Canal group was commissioned to design one for men 500 meters away. From the beginning, architects Patrick and Daniel Rubin established a good rapport with the clothing designer, who would entrust to them a number of other boutiques in Paris and abroad. The basic principle of these designs is to differentiate each boutique from its predecessors by adapting it to its context. Standardization and even a consistent image were abandoned. But a recognizable scheme of colors, materials, and furniture was developed whose character reflects Montana's fondness for airplanes, leather, metal, and fine materials. The small, bluish boutique on the

rue de Grenelle became a "totem" amid the other shops, for it represents a symbolic point in the designer's rise in this fashion capital. The interior space is limited, consisting of only about 45 square meters; it progresses like a long corridor from the street to the dressing rooms. The entire space exists in a state of tension, scored by receding lines, from the oblique false ceiling to the shelves in the shape of airplane wings. The architects left the facade alone, under orders from the Bâtiments de France. Only a discreet, flat sign figures there—a simple vertical blue stripe. In the front window a small "pool" of bright blue powder spread under a sheet of glass focuses attention on a single mannequin. Behind this the

architects have installed a curved glass screen upon which is engraved Montana's signature. To the side, a rigid flag made of the same steel-blue hangs from a chrome-plated pole.
One must progress way past the entrance to discover the clothes, as if the space extended indefinitely. In reality, the effect consists of a tromp l'oeil. The architects have exaggerated what was at first a defect—the considerable depth of the space. Reflections animate the whole: mirrors and glass partitions, smooth or textured stainless-steel floors and structures, and the constellation of small points of light of the ceiling fixtures. Each part of the store was designed down to the smallest details, as are Montana's own creations.

Client: *Claude Montana, fashion designer, Paris.*
Product: *Men's clothing.*
Location: *37, rue de Grenelle, Paris.*
Architects: *Canal: Daniel and Patrick Rubin, with Annie Lebot.*
Date of completion: *1983.*
Materials: *On the floor, slabs of black granite and slivers of granite inserted in the slabs of textured stainless steel, vat of blue powder under glass for the front window, screen of stainless steel and curved glass, shelves in perforated metal and sandblasted glass. Major work for the mirrors: 19mm-thick glass treated by bending, sandblasting, engraving, plating, and beveling. Inset low-voltage halogen spots.*
Floor area: *45 square meters.*
Cost: *Approximately 76,000 dollars.*

1. Length of space designed to convey tension. The walls are covered with "Montana blue" paint and mirrors. The perforated metal shelves have built-in fluorescent lights. The cabinets below house clothing.
2. View of the back of the store. The custom-made table shaped like an airplane wing, made of very thick glass, is attached to the floor. The plaster ceiling inclines slightly to accentuate the tension of this small space. Tiny, inset halogen spotlights (of low voltage) form a constellation of points of light.

PATRICK AND DANIEL RUBIN
CANAL

1. *View of the small front window featuring a divider of curved glass with a steel frame.*
2. *Details of the construction of the Plexiglass flag for the front window.*
3. *Longitudinal section and facade.*
4. *Floor detail. Strips of granite are inserted between slabs of black or textured stainless steel.*
5. *Perforated metal shelves in the shape of airplane wings.*
6. *Detail of black-painted metal clothing racks with steel wings.*
7. *Plan and section.*

1

2

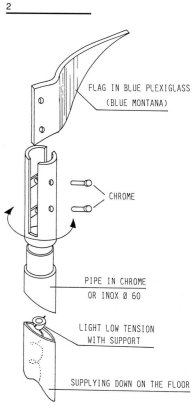

FLAG IN BLUE PLEXIGLASS
(BLUE MONTANA)

CHROME

PIPE IN CHROME
OR INOX Ø 60

LIGHT LOW TENSION
WITH SUPPORT

SUPPLYING DOWN ON THE FLOOR

3

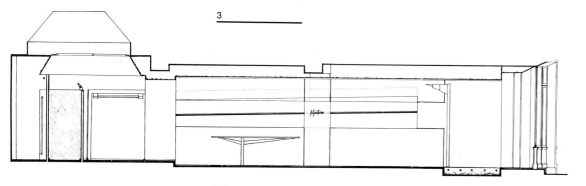

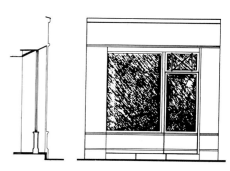

4

5

6

7

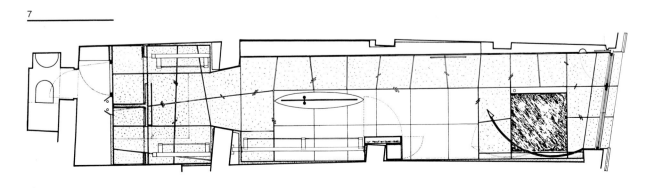
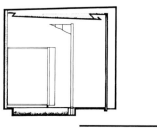

BERNARD FRIC
ASYMÉTRIE

ALFREDO CARAL

MADRID 1986

Fashion designer Alfredo Caral opened his first boutique on one of the trendiest commercial arteries of Madrid. All the big names in Spanish and international design are there, from Adolfo Dominguez to Hermès, Armani, and Saint-Laurent. The Caral boutique is located in a recently restored building dating from 1900 and is adjacent to the Prada and Loewe boutiques, which have the same type of frontage. The designers of the three shops faced the same architectural constraint—they had to preserve the granite of the facade to maintain the building's original character.

The rather classical Caral designs are aimed at a bourgeois Madrid clientele whom they outfit from head to foot: clothes, bags, shoes, accessories, hats, etc. Responding to these givens, the architects of Asymétrie mingled classicism and tradition with eclectic modernism for the new store. They refer as much to Conran's style as to hi-tech. In addition, the curved cutouts of the store's columns and porticos trace silhouettes recalling those of Gaudi.

Rather than adopt the strictures of "gray, black, and white," the designers gave the space a warm and sunny character in harmony with the city's climate. The dominant tone of the light-colored oak floorboards unifies the interior, while the colored elements—the painted plaster partitions and posts—present a range of luminous pastels, from pale yellow to beige, from pinkish beige to ochre, from blue to sea green.

A fervent admirer of Italian architecture and design, Alfredo Caral took a brief trip to Italy with his architects before they began making sketches for the project. He visited the boutiques of Florence and Milan with them to give them some indication of his tastes and preferences.

The store is divided into two parts: the ground floor for women and the basement for men. The two levels are linked by a metal staircase that winds around a large wall punctured by an interior window. With its play of transparencies and reflections, mirrors, and copper or chrome-plated railings, the staircase constitutes the focal point of the design.

Lighting is also accentuated. On the ceiling are indirect fluorescent lights and movable low-voltage halogen spots. The atmosphere changes from natural light on the ground floor to artificial but more intimate lighting in the basement.

Client: *Alfredo Caral, fashion designer, Madrid.*
Products: *Men's and women's clothing, accessories, and shoes.*
Location: *calle Severano, 32, Madrid.*
Architects: *Asymétrie: Bernard Fric with Bruno Rosenweig and Corine Grannet.*
Coordinators: *Angel Sanchez Bernny with Francisco Albano on site.*
Construction: *Adac.*
Signage, logo, packaging: *Minium. Olivier Delecluze, Bernard Baissait, graphic designers.*
Date of completion: *1986.*
Materials: *Floor in white oak and pink marble, partitions in pastel-colored stucco, furniture in aluminum, oak, and copper, bannisters in copper and chrome. The entire store is lit by low-voltage halogen spots and indirect fluorescent ceiling lights.*
Floor area: *500 square meters.*
Cost: *Approximately 300,000 dollars.*

View of the central staircase with white oak steps and copper and chrome bannisters. The focal point of the store, the staircase, is visible from both floors. The halogen spots are of low voltage.

BERNARD FRIC
ASYMÉTRIE

1. Plan of ground floor.
2. Plan of basement.
3. Cross-section.
4. Longitudinal section.
5. Street facade.
6. View of basement. The asymmetrical rounded columns refer to Gaudi.
7. On the ground floor the punctured wall over the stairway is painted a pastel shade.
8. Detail of the furniture: glass-covered accessory showcase with aluminum sides and a wooden body.

1

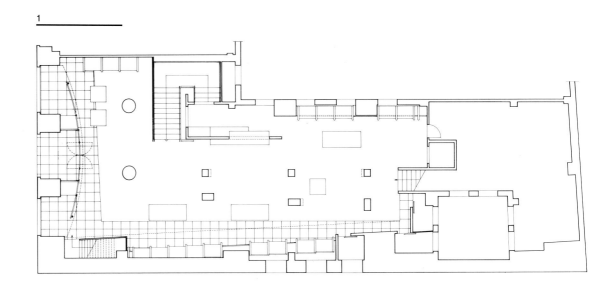

2

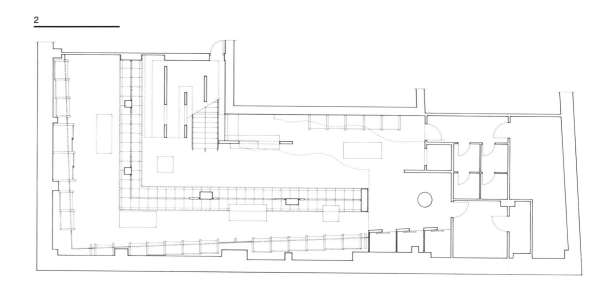

3

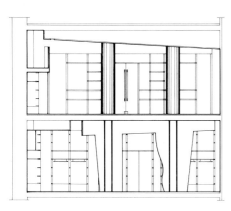

4

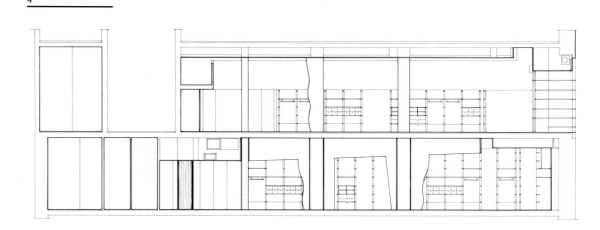

5

6

7

8

DU BESSET
LYON
MORITA

HIROKO KOSHINO

PARIS   1984

The boutique was originally to be designed by Tadao Ando who, finding the distance between Paris and Tokyo too great, suggested to well-known fashion designer Koshino (for whom Ando had already designed a house) that he choose younger colleagues based in Paris. This was a piece of luck for the trio of du Besset, Lyon, and Morita, but became no simple undertaking. During the entire construction process all discussions with the client were carried on between Paris and Tokyo via Telex and telephone. Decisions had to be made quickly because of a shortage of time.

The project is inserted in a nineteenth-century Parisian building in a space characterized by vaulted ceilings and non-orthogonal stone walls. The space previously housed an art gallery with no window on the street front, accessible from an interior courtyard.

The first task was to gut the entire space. The vaulting was demolished. Only the pillars supporting the building remain visible along the facade. These are now aligned behind the glass panes of the shop window—the minimum requirement of the Bâtiments de France. On the interior of these irregular walls the architects created a sort of box detached from the existing structure to establish a new geometric order. This is a cubic volume (aligned with the facade) whose nine-square grid is marked on the floor and ceiling and whose members are made of rose and Indian grey granite. The stuccoed walls unify the space.

The old, chaotic passageway that connected the art gallery to the street has been made into the scheme's most original element. It now serves as a transition corridor between two sales areas, one for clothes and one for shoes. It was designed in imitation of the footbridges of No theater and treated in section as an immense, regular curve. The arc of the footbridge is divided by a line between the stone and carpeting. Another arc appears on the wall.

The choice and combination of materials throughout the boutique is refined; the gray, rose and beige paint and the curves and cubes of the space clearly suggest the spirit of modern Japan. The cubic rear volume is naturally lit by a glass door opening onto the courtyard.

Client: *Hiroko Koshino, fashion designer, Tokyo.*
Products: *Women's clothing.*
Architects: *Pierre du Besset, Dominique Lyon, Kazutoshi Morita.*
Date of completion: *1984.*
Materials: *Perforated metal borders and steps, granite gridding on stone flooring, granite and plaster ceiling, pink and Indian gray granite pillars, stucco walls, perforated gray metal display cases and tables.*
Floor area: *140 square meters.*
Cost: *300,000 dollars (including furniture), of which 60,000 dollars went to major construction (demolition of the vaulting, construction of a new floor, etc.).*

General view of ground floor. The cubic volume detached from the existing walls is marked by a nine-square grid with a series of beams around the periphery. The whole structure is made of pink and Indian gray marble. The grid is taken up again on the floor and ceiling.

1

1. Corridor scored with a pattern of curves. The shelf mounted on the wall is of perforated metal. The light walls are painted stucco.
2. View of ground floor facing shelves.
3. Detail of bannister.
4. Axonometric.
5. Plan.

4

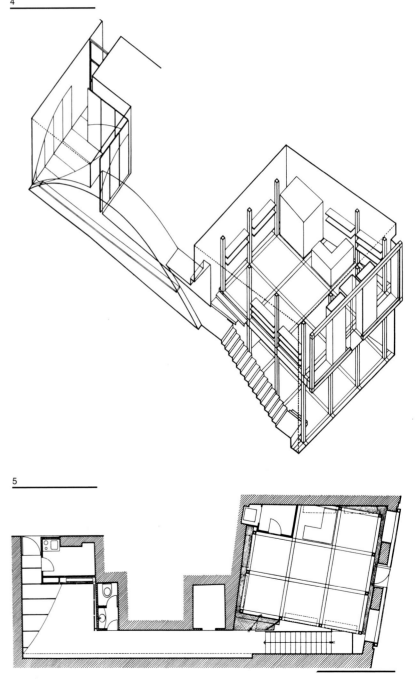

5

69

JEAN-LOUIS VÉRET
GÉRARD RONZATTI

SHU UEMURA

PARIS   1986

Shu Uemura or the art of beauty: behind this name hides one of the most respected cosmetic professionals of Japan. His style has a following both in Japan and around the world. Before entering business, this exceptional artist had a long career in film, notably in the United States, where since the fifties he has been the make-up artist for major Hollywood feature films. His expertise led him to create in 1967 a cosmetics firm that soon expanded to include beauty and facial products. By 1987, the Shu Uemura company included three subsidiaries and forty-three franchises worldwide. The general concept of all the boutiques consists of emphasizing the artistic and aesthetic rather than the clinical aspects of the cosmetics. The environments are to be sober, effective, and elegant, so that the products become the main attraction: an infinite range of colors in transparent containers.

The Parisian boutique was conceived in this spirit, with the same graphics, logo, and packaging as the other stores. But this shop distinguishes itself from the rest by its architecture, providing a scenario appropriate to the Parisian context. The project is based on an urbanistic strategy; the architects sought to integrate the shop into the life of the quarter by articulating the relationship between public and private spaces. An interior "street" continues the sidewalk and boulevard Saint-Germain through an intermediary geometric form—the cylinder—which serves as the major emblem of the scheme.

Inspired by Palladio's theater in Vicenza, Jean-Louis Véret has created a small theater whose permanent interior decor offers a new spectacle to passersby at each moment. The lights, of adjustable intensity, permit modification and accentuation of the "sets" at different hours of the day. The designers have achieved an ambiance close to that of movie and theater set designs. The first of its kind in Paris, the Saint-Germain-des-Prés boutique illustrates the Japanese mastery of the arts of cosmetics and beauty.

Client: *Shu Uemura, Tokyo.*
Products: *Beauty products and cosmetics.*
Location: *176, boulevard Saint-Germain, Paris.*
Architects: *Jean-Louis Véret and Gérard Ronzatti.*
Date of completion: *1986.*
Materials: *Floor of slabs of Spanish gray granite, central element and cashier's desk in pickled ash, divider of glassblock, shelves of brushed stainless steel with attached fluorescent lights, cylinder in black anodized aluminum with wooden grillwork inside, fluorescent tubing for the mirrors, low-voltage halogen bulbs of adjustable intensity for the cylinder.*
Floor area: *120 square meters.*
Cost: *Approximately 300,000 dollars.*

View of main space used for reception, sales, and demonstration of products. The interior of the cylindrical volume is a wooden grillwork incorporating the store's only lighting, which is of adjustable intensity.

JEAN-LOUIS VÉRET
GÉRARD RONZATTI

1. Facade at night.
2. Presentation of products: a series of transparent boxes of make-up are systematically arranged on the side wall of the boutique. The shelves are of industrial steel with built-in fluorescent lights.
3. View from the back of the store, facing the entrance. The wall opposite the shelves is of light-green pickled wood.
4. Preparation of products. This space, not visible from the entrance, is reserved for beauty treatments.
5. Axonometric.

1

2

3

4

5

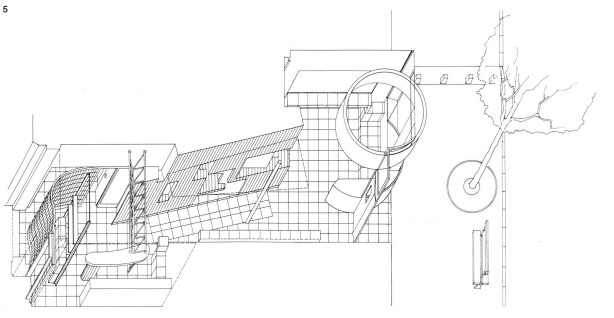

MAURICE MARTY
PATRICK LE HUÉROU

JEAN-PAUL GAULTIER

PARIS   1986

Maurice Marty and Patrick Le Huérou conceived fashion designer Jean-Paul Gaultier's showroom by entering into a game with his style and fantasies. There was a formidable give and take of ideas, further stimulated by the site, which offered many possibilities for design. The structure was originally a marionette theater, built in 1930, of considerable size—40 meters deep, 7 meters wide, and 6.5 meters high—with an enormous skylight. In sum, it provided an ideal environment in which to situate Gaultier's originality and to design a boutique matching his image. Once the project was completed, clothing and architecture combined in an unlikely mix of styles and periods. Jean-Paul Gaultier wanted a decidedly Western architecture, but one out of the ordinary, "the weight of tradition, the shock of the new." To satisfy this desire, the architects created a baroque space reflecting the designer's taste. They pay homage to Eiffel and to the style of the Paris metro stations, make use of videos (omnipresent in their architecture), and yet manage to nod to Roman classicism.

Eiffel's influence is seen in the sinuous staircases and immense decorative metal porticos that frame and punctuate the main circulation path. Everything from the dressing rooms to the cashier's desk, display cases, and clothing racks was conceived in glass and verdigris metal recalling the old metro stations.

To complete the decor, the architects installed a series of old red velvet theater seats on the second floor. From the balcony of this floor one can view the floor below, composed of fragments of ceramic in concrete. Into this mosaic, recreated in the mode of Pompeii, the designers inserted circular steel video portholes that show clips of Gaultier fashion shows. These are also projected onto a screen measuring 1.5 by 2 meters and attached to the ceiling by means of a bellows camera (3 meters in length) that can advance, recede, and turn on automatically. To accentuate the scenographic affect, several large, disjointed marionettes dressed in Gaultier outfits pose in each corner of the room. The architects would have liked to have made these function like true automatons (which they originally were) to surprise customers. These set-designing architects have still obtained their objective: spectacle is everywhere.

Clients: *Jean-Paul Gaultier and Francis Ménuge, under the sponsorship of Kashiyama France group.*
Products: *Men's and women's clothing.*
Location: *6, rue Vivienne, Paris.*
Architects: *Design Environment: Maurice Marty and Patrick Le Huérou.*
Date of completion: *1986.*
Floor area: *Approximately 400 square meters.*
Cost: *1,500,000 dollars for the whole (offices and showroom are in the same building); approximately 150,000 dollars for the video equipment, which amounts to a virtual video studio.*

General view showing both levels of the store, as seen from the ground floor under the art deco skylight. Symmetrical staircases lead from both sides up to the mezzanine level. The portholes embedded in the floor project films of Jean-Paul Gaultier fashion shows on small round screens.

**MAURICE MARTY
PATRICK LE HUÉROU**

1. Second floor. The old velvet theater seats are installed in front of the office space, closed off by glass walls and doors.
2. Plan of second floor.
3. Disjointed automaton transformed into a mannequin.
4. Side staircases.
5. Stairway leading to the offices, which are not accessible to the public.
6. Ground floor plan.

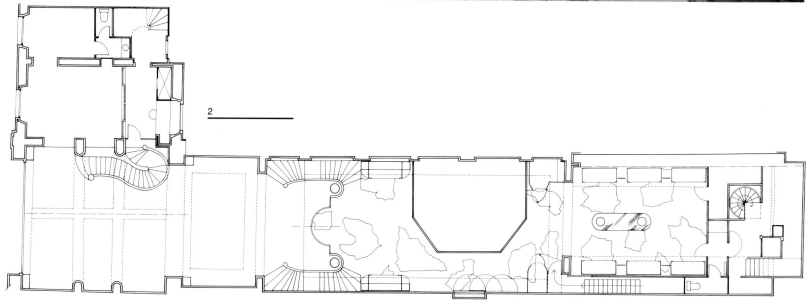

3

4

5

6

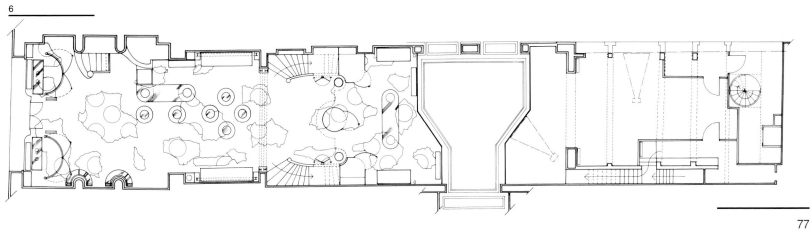

**MAURICE MARTY
PATRICK LE HUÉROU**

1. Detail of large electronic clock.
2. View down from the mezzanine.
3. View of closed display cases on the mezzanine level. This space under the second half of the skylight was conceived as a covered gallery.

JIRICNA KERR ASSOCIATES

JOSEPH POUR LA VILLE
LONDON   1986

Main proponent of an aesthetic halfway between hi-tech and art deco, Eva Jiricna has designed some of London's most stylish interiors since 1981. Thanks to her fetishist client Joseph Ettedgui, for whom she has designed apartments, boutiques, a cafe, and a restaurant, she could express her notion of stripped-down space and impose the "metallic black" style now emblematic of Joseph. Jiricna's modernist sensibility, which rejects ostentation, imbues her designs with an unmistakable personality that has engendered a whole series of imitators smitten by her "black and white" look. This wild success has propelled her into the international design scene.

Joseph pour la ville is the fourth such boutique that Eva Jiricna has designed. The first—Joseph Tricot—was built in 1983. Here she refines and reinforces the use of chrome-plated metal.

But all of her projects share a single sales concept, of which her client is a pioneer in England: "minimal presentation." This Japanese style transforms the display of goods into an exhibition; from the street the whole boutique resembles one big shop window.

In Joseph pour la ville it was necessary to open up the basement onto the main space so that the store's two levels would be visible from outside. Jiricna employed a balustrade transparent enough not to disrupt the perspective from above but sufficiently conspicuous to guide the viewer's gaze to the area below. A third level, not visible from the ground floor, is intended for the display of furniture and household items. To accentuate the depth of the space, Jiricna exploited its narrowness, installing mirrors on the back wall of the shop and grouping the entrance doors, staircase, skylight, and cashier's desk on a single axis. The boutique is designed with great rigor, as is usual for Jiricna, but most of the elements designed here are more curvaceous and sophisticated in their detailing than usual. The doorknobs, railings, furniture hardware, and staircase nosing are of a unique pattern and their surfaces are chrome-plated. Her palette remains invariably monochromatic and her materials industrial: glass, steel, metal marine cables, portholes, terrazzo, and plaster.

Client: *Joseph Ettedgui, London.*
Products: *Men's and women's clothing, household items.*
Location: *268, Brompton Road, London.*
Architects: *Jiricna Kerr Associates: Eva Jiricna assisted by Alan Morris.*
Engineers: *Dewhurst MacFarlane and Partners.*
Date of completion: *1986.*
Materials: *Gray-tinted maple for the floors, Sigmulto for the walls, sheets of cast steel for the staircase nosing, sections of industrial glass for the shelves, low-voltage metal iodide spots for the upper level, halogen lamps with low-voltage spots for the basement level.*
Floor area: *150 square meters (including second floor).*
Cost: *Approximately 260,000 dollars.*

General view of the store. On the entrance axis, across the stairwell with its chrome-plated railings, one sees the basement. The skylight, on axis above the staircase, has a black metal structure with frosted glass panes and is artificially lit. The floorboards are tinted gray.

1

1. *View of the facade at night. The entire boutique is visible from the outside. There is no front display window; the entire space functions as a display case.*
2. *Plan.*

2

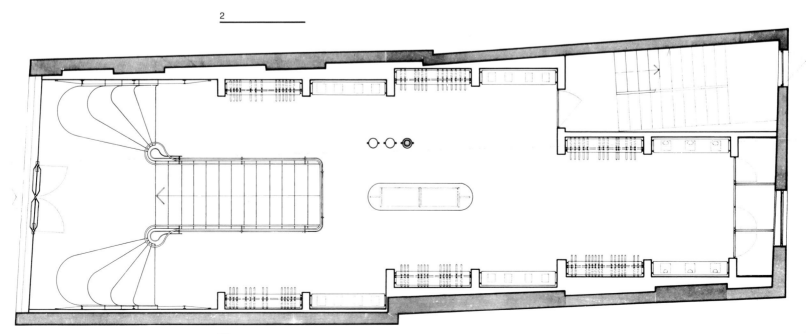

3

4

3. The clothes are hung on steel cables mounted on white walls. The nosing of the side staircases is made of fine layers of cast iron.
4. View of second floor, on the cash register side.
5. Longitudinal section.

5

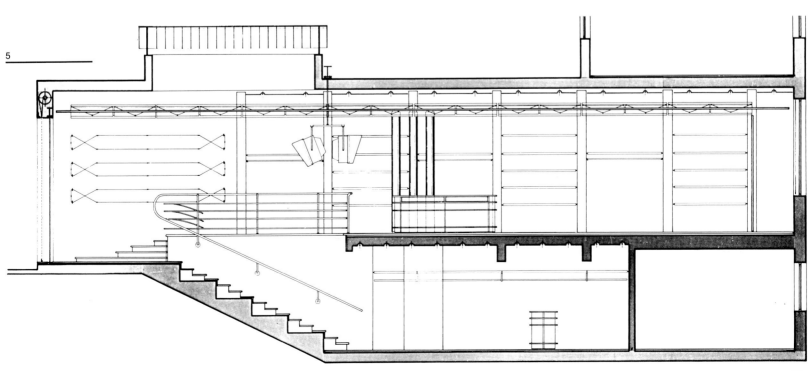

**DAVID CHIPPERFIELD
KENNETH ARMSTRONG**

ISSEY MIYAKE

LONDON   1985

A disciple of the English hi-tech school, David Chipperfield distinguishes himself from it by a more rational architecture without superfluous stylistic touches. Influenced by the work of Carlo Scarpa, he seeks to achieve in his projects a similar sensuality and attention to detail and composition.

The Issey Miyake boutique in London gave Chipperfield and Kenneth Armstrong the chance to express their penchant for beautiful materials and almost imperceptible detail. The shop replaces the old Miyake boutique (located on the same site) which had been designed using typical Japanese cliches such as black-tinted wood beams and heaps of "artistic" pebbles and wood chips. For the new scheme, the two English architects wanted to avoid such literal cultural references.

The boutique is divided into two spaces marked by different ceiling heights. The tight space was compensated for by reducing lines and surfaces, all rendered in natural materials of warm colors. A marble wall contrasts with the rough wood floor and the reception area bench, thus marking the border between this space and the one in the rear used for trying on clothes. The whole is composed of few elements: a single long metal clothing rack, groups of dressing rooms at the back, and a display element in metal and sculpted wood. According to Chipperfield, "The most luxurious thing one can have in a clothing store is a wall free of clothing."

While making reference to Scarpa, the architects also evoke the image of modern Japan in tune with Miyake's designs. At the present time, Miyake is one of the major fashion designers both in his own country and abroad. His designs are cut in simple geometric shapes. Admiring this method, Chipperfield and Armstrong decided to adopt a similar approach for the shop design. Their main concern was not to design a stylish interior but rather to create a harmonious space realized in simple, even "poor" materials. To this end they sought the clarity of Japanese architecture while avoiding caricature. They wished to evoke a spirit rather than present a "look."

Client: *Issey Miyake International, Tokyo.*
Products: *Women's clothing.*
Location: *Sloane Street, London.*
Architects: *David Chipperfield and Kenneth Armstrong.*
Associated Architects: *David Gomersall and Sally Greaves-Lord.*
Undulating table: *John Harwood.*
Date of completion: *1985.*
Materials: *Undulating wood table in sycamore, Portland stone, rough wood, and marble.*
Floor area: *Approximately 70 square meters.*

The minimalist space was designed lengthwise, with juxtaposed materials marking different zones: rough and natural wood for the reception area, gray-veined white marble for the back wall. The two spaces are differentiated by differing ceiling heights.

1. Plan.
2. Axonometric.

1

2

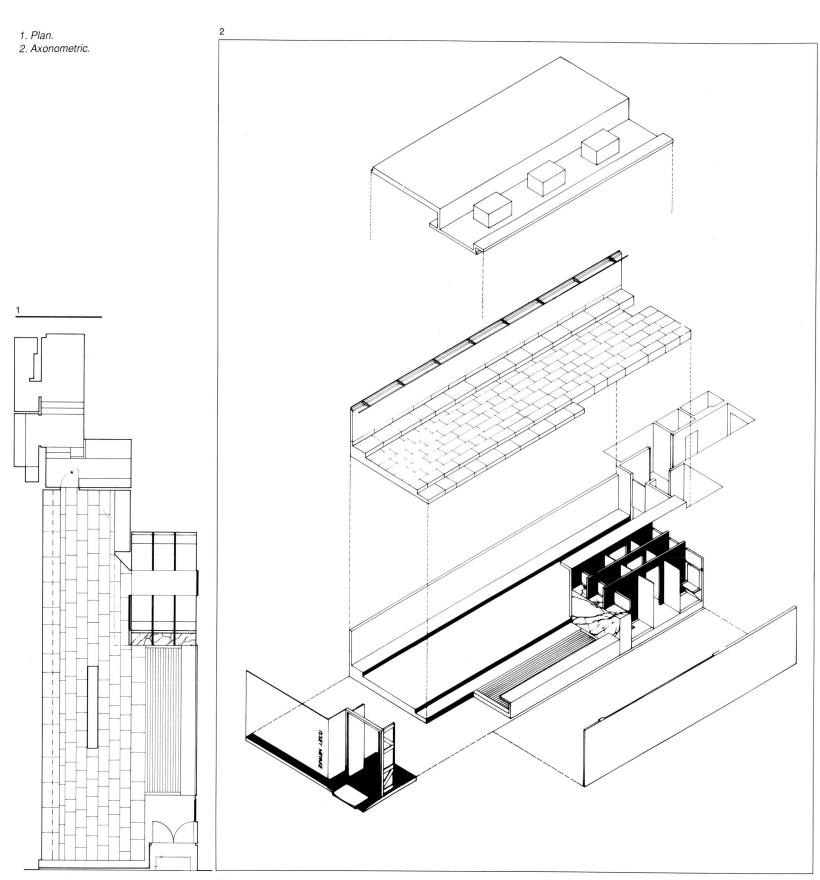

3

4

3. Light wood bench.
4. Solid wood sculpted table with a base of slender shafts of black-painted metal, built by John Harwood.
5. View from outside, at night. The boutique was designed as a long platform to accommodate fashion shows. There is no front window per se.

5

FOSTER ASSOCIATES

KATHERINE HAMNETT
LONDON 1986

Only Norman Foster would conceive of a boutique without a trace of a shop window; only Katherine Hamnett would agree that the only signal on the street front should be a sign bearing her name, without a trace of clothing. This fashion designer, well known in London for her "casual chic" creations, can allow herself this extravagance, intended to please and arouse the curiosity of her shoppers—a nonconformist clientele who often make no distinction between day and evening clothes beyond certain invariable details. This striking shop was altered from its original function—a garage—to serve as a boutique. It belongs to that new species of spaces—the loft—much prized by Hamnett's clientele.

"Conveniently located, the garage possessed no entrance facade; one entered by way of a dark passage. To envision a front window was thus impossible. It was like a two-story rabbit hole, which seemed, however, to provide great spatial possibilities. The challenge was to restore the space to its lost grandeur and, at the same time, respect the constraints of time and money. In the beginning, the only manner of perceiving the whole was to construct a large model of the "skeleton" without the intermediate flooring. The trick was to "sew up" a sort of new steel lacework while improving the quality of the existing structure, conserving, for example, the full height of the cast-iron columns. "If the space itself was a major concern, the quality of light was another. The place is lighted by a combination of side lights—old industrial windows reglazed with opaque glass, producing a translucent effect—and of overhead lights in the form of skylights in the roof. At night the ceiling lights illuminate from the outside in; they create a background lighting to which is added, on the interior, the light of movable lamps on tracks that reinforce the structural geometry of the space.

"The entrance, not so long ago an amorphous tunnel, is today completely transformed by the introduction of a single element: a glass bridge lit from below with neon . . . an attempt to evoke mystery, contrast, and drama." (Notes by Norman Foster, 1986).

Client: *Katherine Hamnett, fashion designer, London.*
Products: *Designer clothing for men and women.*
Location: *264 Brompton Road, London.*
Architects: *Foster Associates.*
Date of completion: *December 1986.*
Materials: *Concrete floor, slabs of opaque industrial glass for the bridge with fluorescent tubing below, cashier's desk and display cases in frosted glass, movable track lights.*
Floor area: *500 square meters for the boutique, 50 square meters for storage, and 85 square meters for the corridor.*

View of the showroom's large entrance doorway. After crossing the glass bridge one reaches this immense, stripped-down space. The structural framework was painted white and strengthened by supporting members. The skylight, patterned in translucent glass, is lit from the outside at night. The dressing rooms at the back are hidden behind large mirrored partitions that exaggerate the depth of the space.

1. Preliminary sketch.
2. View of the lighted bridge made of sheets of industrial glass lit from below by fluorescent tubes.
3. Sketch of facade.
4. Axonometric.
5. Interior elevation.

2

KATHARINE HAMNETT

1

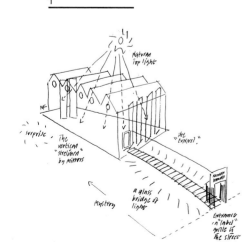

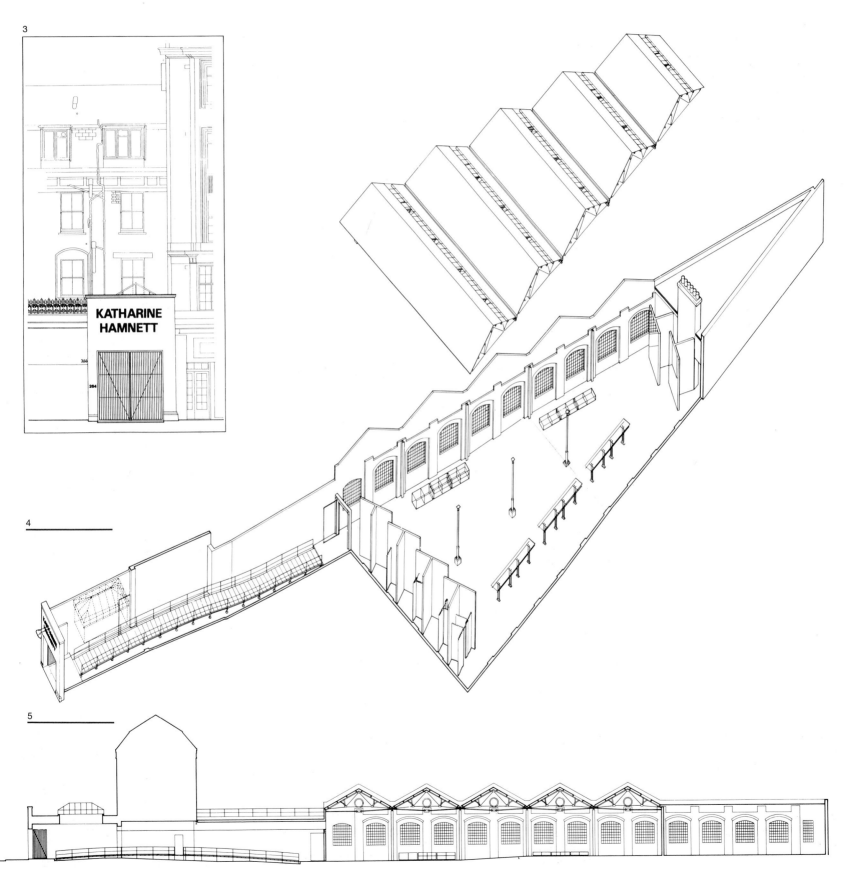

3

KATHARINE
HAMNETT

4

5

1

1. The showroom as reflected in mirrors at the back.
2. Reflection of the roof.
3. Dressing rooms.

TAKAO KAWASAKI

COMME DES GARÇONS
NEW YORK   1983

A leader in her own way of the brutalist tendency, fashion designer Ray Kawabuko, with Comme des garçons, was one of the first in the late seventies to transmit an avant-garde image of her country to the West. One could say that she is at the root of westerners' infatuation with Japanese style and design, which in its extremes ranges from formalism to snobbery.

Her showrooms are now spread around the world and have an unmistakable identity. Missing are any superfluous colors and motifs; folklore and tradition have given way to an extreme form of modernism. Her clothes are rigorous and without ostentation—remarkable for the geometry of their lines, the beauty of their materials, and their at first imperceptible extravagance, expressed in the details of the pleating, the asymmetrical hemlines, the monochromatic combinations of black,

marine blue, anthracite, and white.

The spaces resemble the clothes. Born of minimalist ideas that are then minutely orchestrated, they suggest scenarios of "emptiness and understatement." Kawabuko controls everything in her austere universe; clothes, space, and even music are synthesized. The spaces conserve the innate sense of emptiness and of the Japanese arts of exhibition and assemblage. Everything here seems to subscribe to the new religion of "nothing in excess," not even a ticket hanging from the end of a sleeve. New York's Soho boutique is actually one of Comme des garçon's most beautiful spaces, even though it was one of the first to be designed. It is one that best reflects this "anti-luxury" approach—a provocative gesture of the chic toward a coarse, almost "poor" look. This is also the first shop to present the entire

collection under one roof, with women's clothing on the ground floor and men's clothing in the basement.

The two levels are visible on the facade. In order to give the sense of a single space, the architect centered the main staircase and created an enormous stairwell to provide the largest possible opening. The visual effect of this apparent "vacuum," with its concrete walls, floors, and shelves, is striking. By means of its neutral surfaces it highlights atmospheric contrasts. Whereas most architects seek natural light, here the designer did away with the existing skylight—not just to affect the colors of the mostly somber clothes, but also to either soften or intensify their contours by means of movable spotlights. The entire area of the store is given over to the display of clothing and provides a truly scenographic background.

Client: *Comme des garçons, Tokyo.*
Products: *Men's and women's clothing.*
Location: *Wooster Street, Soho, New York.*
Conception: *Ray Kawabuko.*
Design: *Takao Kawasaki (Strawberry Fields).*
Construction: *Howard Reitzes.*
Date of completion: *1983.*
Materials: *Concrete for the walls, floors shelves, and benches. 3-meter by 8-meter display tables of black-painted wood joists, top of cashier's desk in laminated oak painted black with metal corners, balustrade of rectangular tubing, shelves of chrome-plated steel, black-painted steel frame for facade.*
Floor area: *585 square meters: 340 on the ground floor, 245 in the basement.*

The space is completely stripped down. The walls and floors are of untreated concrete. On the first floor, two large display pieces in varnished rough wood, with inclined surfaces, extend across almost the entire width of the store. A single garment is displayed here, illustrating the Japanese art of presentation.

1. Axonometric.
2. Longitudinal section.
3. The basement was also designed with few elements: a concrete bench, a leather armchair by Eileen Grey. The shelves are in untreated concrete and the custom-made table is in glass and steel.

1
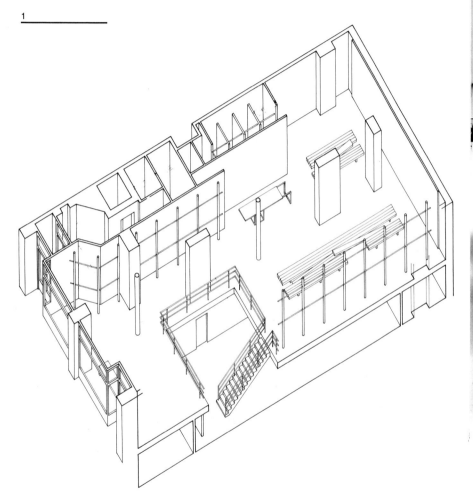

3

2
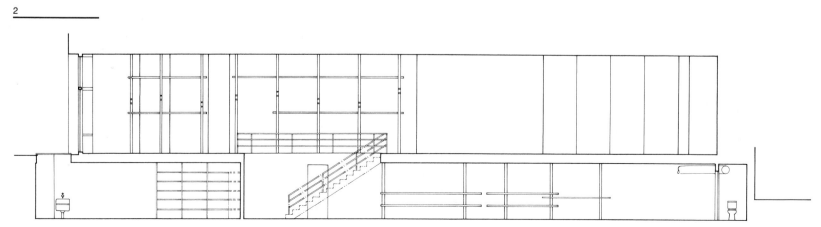

4

4. Ground floor, view of the central staircase volume. The railings are made of black metal.
5. Sketch of furniture: the cashier's desk.
6. Sketch of the air conditioning system above the dressing rooms.

5

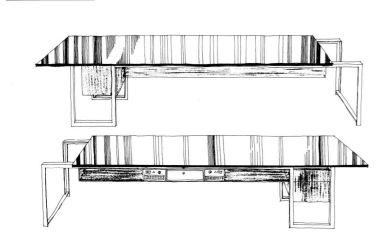

6

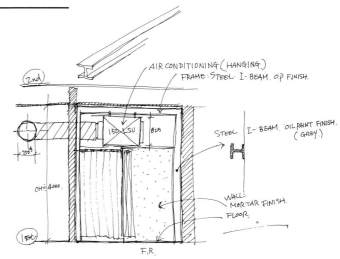

97

SITE

WILLIWEAR FOR MEN
NEW YORK   1982

From the earliest discussions of the future Williwear showroom, designer Willi Smith expressed a desire to show his clothes in a context resembling New York's streets rather than in a traditional couture salon. This provided an excellent occasion for Site designers to express their taste for the spectacular in exploiting a surreal mingling of interior and exterior.

The design of the showroom transforms a former warehouse, whose rudimentary aspect was conserved both for effect and to stay within the limits of the tight budget. The whole was conceived as a collage of urban fragments made entirely of found objects: bricks, stones, tin cans, water pipes, fire hydrants, chain-link fencing, smokestacks, sidewalk garbage cans, etc. The entire interior, including the movable elements, was painted a uniform light gray in order to blur the episodic nature of the individual elements and to create a neutral backdrop for the display of colorful clothing. The fences and pipes provide a practical system for hanging garments—a stylized *prêt-à-porter*.

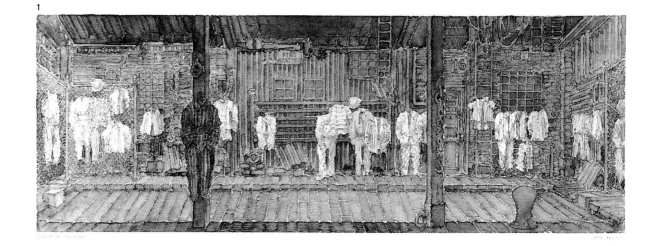

1

Client: *Williwear, New York.*
Products: *Men's clothing.*
Location: *209 West 38th Street, New York.*
Architects: *Site Projects: James Wines, Allison Sky, Michelle Stone.*
Date of completion: *1982.*
Floor area: *Approximately 700 square meters.*

1. Sketch.
2. Interior of showroom. All of the decor is along the periphery on a narrow wood platform intended for fashion shows. All of the elements found on the street— chain-link fencing, garbage cans, fire hydrants, pipes, etc.—are used for displays as well as decoration. They were all painted a uniform shade of gray.

SHIRO KURAMATA

ISSEY MIYAKE SEIBU
TOKYO   1987

This curious space, entirely realized in metal meshing, is located inside of Seibu, one of Tokyo's most sophisticated department stores. Like most large Japanese commercial interiors, Seibu is a conglomerate of individual showrooms quite different in nature from the ordinary concept of street front boutiques. In Seibu, boutiques are juxtaposed, with each one asserting its particular identity. Fashion designer Issey Miyake commissioned his friend Shiro Kuramata, who had designed most of his other boutiques, to compose this "corner." Respected in Japan for his highly designed interiors, Kuramata has to his credit over 300 boutiques and restaurants as well as an entire line of furniture considered to epitomize avant-garde design. Since the 1970's he has been admired and imitated by the young generation of Japanese designers, who consider him to be the master of contemporary design. This great designer works like an artist while willfully remaining in the realm of the concrete and the real. He attempts to evoke in his projects "a state of weightlessness" that defies the laws of statics and of equilibrium. To reach the essential and express the trace of time, he gives to his spaces or objects the effect of "interiority and spirituality" by reducing as much as possible their physical materiality. His essentially minimalist creations, like that at Seibu, resonate with metallic vibrations. Shadows and lights play across a space of lightweight, transparent structures. Kuramata conceives of the design of the "immaterial"— from the visible to the invisible— by integrating light and matter. Yet he does not neglect an element of humor that leads him to create droll and expressive forms. It is not surprising to learn that in the Seibu boutique the extensive use of metal meshing exacerbates the sensation of emptiness and the limits of fullness. Yet this metallic net circumscribes a palpable space that asserts itself as a discrete entity within the larger store.

Client: *Issey Miyake International.*
Products: *Men's clothing.*
Location: *Seibu Department Store Building B, 1F21-1 Utagawa-Mchi, Shibuya-Ku, Tokyo.*
Architect: *Shiro Kuramata.*
Construction: *Ishimaru (management). Terada Ironworks (metalwork).*
Date of completion: *February 18, 1987.*
Materials: *400 square meters of mixed gravel for the floor. Partitions and ceilings in black-painted metal meshing. Shelves in chrome-plated metal openwork. Storage and display elements in brushed aluminum.*
Floor area: *78 square meters.*

The showroom is located within the Seibu department store. Made entirely of metal meshing, the showroom opens onto the central passageway.

SHIRO KURAMATA

1. Axonometric.
2. Side view of the metal vaulting.
3. General view. The space measures
approximately 80 square meters.
4. Detail of display elements.
5. Cross-section.

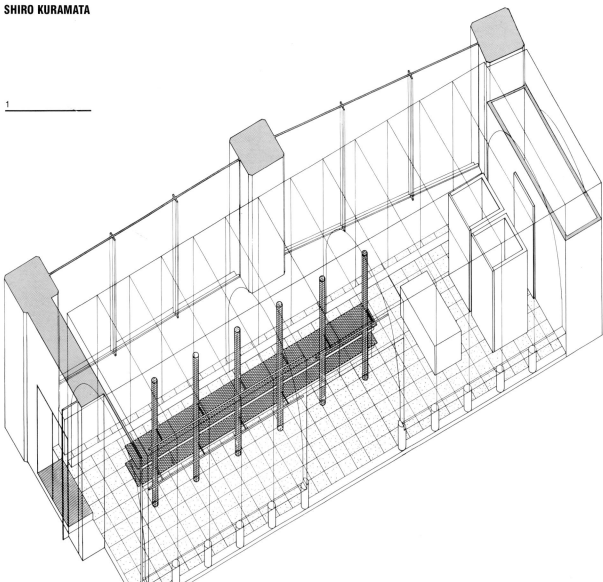

4

5

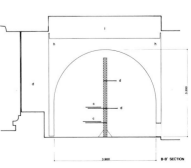

B-B' SECTION

SHIRO KURAMATA

ISSEY MIYAKE
KOBE   1986

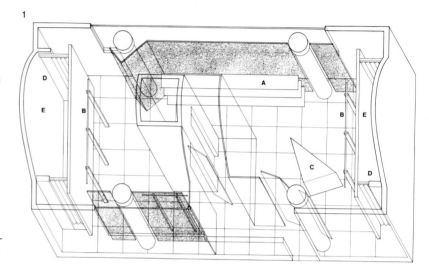

In his designs, Shiro Kuramata reveals his discovery of certain materials. By multiplying their uses (as do many artists at certain periods during their careers) he marks in time the evolution of his work. Man-made materials generally respond best to such manipulation, thanks to the numerous possibilities for their technological applications. Kuramata exploits materials to transform the rigid nature of construction into something playful and, in all of his work, to create images that are as seductive as they are innovative. During a period of infatuation in design with plastic materials, Kuramata worked—always according to his notion of "immateriality"—in Plexiglass. After that he preferred terrazzo (concrete mixed with bits of colored glass), which he used to design tables for Memphis and boutiques for Miyake and Esprit. In recent years he has become obsessed with metal meshing and aluminum netting, as well as with polished black granite.

In the Kobe department store, Kuramata unveils the mysteries of transparency, employing triple-thickness glass that looks like it has been etched but in fact has been carefully cracked—a process that only he and his craftsmen understand or, at least, know how to execute.

Client: *Issey Miyake International.*
Products: *Designer clothing for women.*
Location: *Rilans Gate. Building 4F, 2-4-24, Yamamoto-Dori, Chuou-Ku, Kobe-Shi, Hyougo.*
Interior Design: *Kuramata Design Office.*
Architect: *Tadao Ando Architect and Associates.*
Construction: *Ishimaru (glasswork).*
Date of completion: *April 28, 1986.*
Materials: *Transparent terrazzo with plastic joints for the floor, Formica Colorcore for the partitions, cement ceiling given a coat of paint to modify its color. The transparent screen is made of three layers of reinforced cracked glass.*
Floor area: *102 square meters.*

1. Axonometric.
2. A second Miyake boutique, installed in the Kobe department store. The translucent wall is made of three sheets of glass struck at the middle, creating a sort of ribbed effect similar to etched glass.

MASAKI MORITA

INOUE SACS
TOKYO 1986

Little inspired by the minimalist and conceptualist trend in Japanese design, Masaki Morita has invented a personal language to escape the ranks of imitators of Shiro Kuramata, who was for a long time his guiding influence. His aesthetic rather than pragmatic approach is tied to the poetry of water, stones, flowers, and trees—to all that is inscribed in time. He is greatly influenced by natural forms and by the traditional aesthetics of his country. His interiors align themselves closely and symbolically with that tradition, making distinct reference to ikebana (the Japanese art of flower arranging), which sets flowers in the context of the sky, earth, and mankind. There are

also possible allusions to the Zen pavilions whose rock gardens leave themselves open to the interpretations of each visitor, and thus hover in the zones of mystery. Modernity appears in Morita's use of materials and colors, and in his stylistic twists. The Inoue sacs boutique belongs to a well-known Japanese leather designer who owns about twenty such shops throughout Japan. Located in a department store, the shop is one of six Tokyo franchises designed by Morita. The design is symmetrical, with a rigor characteristic of many Japanese architects. Shelves for displaying handbags were installed on each side; the rest of the arrangement heightens the typical commercial setting by

evoking an atmosphere of mystery. At the center of this highly designed little space, interrupting its emptiness, an enormous cone descends from the ceiling. The cone's artificial light symbolizes a sky obscured by clouds; its shape masks its technical supports. The floor of the boutique, covered in veined marble, is a flat surface symbolizing the earth, while the water—the other basic element—is represented by a small sheet of illuminated glass. At the back of the boutique three large screens rotate, alternately revealing mirrors and opaque surfaces. This elementary symbolism gives the boutique a surprising, unreal atmosphere.

Client: *Inoue sacs.*
Products: *Handbags and leather goods.*
Location: *One-oh-nine Building, 3F, 26-6 Udagawa-Cho Shibuya-Ku, Tokyo.*
Architect: *Design, Masaki Morita.*
Date of completion: *1986.*
Materials: *Walls and floors covered in cream-colored acrylic paint. Floor of white marble and mustard-colored concrete (made of a new blend). Shelves of the same concrete as the floor, with built-in indirect lighting. Cone in aluminum. The three screens are coated with sandblasted concrete.*
Floor area: *48 square meters.*
Cost: *Approximately 56,000 dollars.*

Inoue sacs is a "corner" installed in a Tokyo department store. Three removable screens, opaque on one side and mirrored on the other, form the back of the boutique. The steel cone that occupies the middle of the room is attached to the false ceiling. It provides light while concealing the technical network above. Below it lies a symbolic rendering of water, a circular sheet of frosted glass.

1

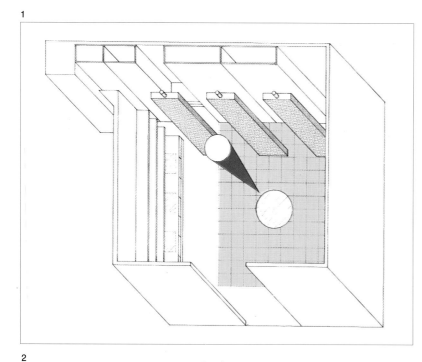

2

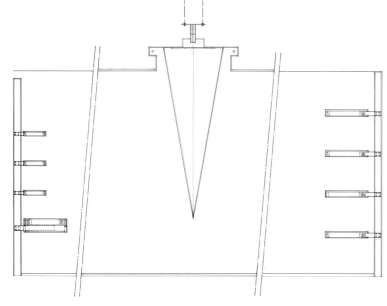

3

4

5

1. Axonometric.
2. Section detail of the display shelves (with their built-in lighting) and of the conical form.
3. Exterior of the boutique from within the department store.
4. View of interior.
5. Symbolic scene-setting: the metal cone is covered with a white cloth to represent clouds. Water, earth, and flowers group themselves beneath the sky.

FURNITURE AND DETAILS

There are no minor problems in designing a showroom. The organization of the shop must take into account the layout and creation of spaces. Whatever its dimensions, a showroom's quality lies in the attention given to details and furnishings. Today the space traditionally reserved for the front display window is treated in such a way that the entire showroom can be seen from the outside. Hence the display of products becomes fundamental. The furniture participates as much in creating varied scenarios as in highlighting the goods. It must be carefully designed and often responds to specific functional requirements. Most showrooms require a cashier's desk, shelves, clothing racks, mirrors, screens, and lights, and few designers choose ready-made furniture. Certain designers, such as Citterio and Kuramata, conceive the furniture, which is then built by others. This gives them a chance to design "to measure" everything from doorknobs to lamps. They do not hesitate to use fine materials or those made available by the most recent technology: pickled oak, brass, copper, marble, glass of all types, polished granite, knotted wood, granito, steel, aluminum, sheet metal or perforated metal, carbon fiber. Built by craftsmen, these often complex and costly prototypes cannot usually be made for commercial sale. True feats of artistic and technological prowess, they are sometimes so well made that they are more desirable than the goods they display. There are several ways to approach the furniture problem. Many architects are categorical; according to them, furniture must be integrated into the decor and harmoniously proportioned. Gropius wrote, "Proportion is one of the functions of the spiritual world: materials and construction are its supports. Proportion tied to an object's function proclaims besides that function its spiritual reason, which transcends utilitarian considerations."[1] If the furniture is successfully ensconced in the interior architecture, it confers on the whole equilibrium, proportion, and harmony. Because of its functional contours, the architecture itself becomes furniture. The "glass house" is one of the milestones of this method of proceeding.

Thus, shelves form volumes; benches and even the cashier's desk become walls and floors. Finally, the details put the final touch on these compact glazed "boxes." The stairway railing, the shield over each sconce, and the doorknob participate in the indispensable refinement of the space's uniqueness.

[1] Walter Gropius, Architectures en Allemagne 1900–1933, cf. Bibliography.

Floor lamps, Shullin II, produced by Baleri (Italy). The columns are made of painted aluminum tubes with a veneer of carrara white marble. The projectors are made of aluminum alloy with 300-watt halogen bulbs.

Sales desk, Williwear Willismith, made of wood and reinforced concrete.

Stainless steel clothing rack, Christophe Lebourg.

Cashier's desk, Shullin II, made of exotic red wood.

Stainless steel tubing clothing racks and transparent glass shelves, Katherine Hamnett.

Oak, aluminum, brass, and glass display case, Alfredo Caral.

Black and white marble table, Fausto Santini.

Cashier's desk, Teresa Ramallal, Barcelona, made of glass, chrome-plated metal tubing, and white stone.

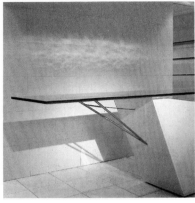

Shoe holder inserted in the floor in the Teresa Ramallal showroom in Barcelona, made of chrome-plated metal.

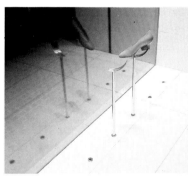

Mahogany display element, Teresa Ramallal, Madrid.

Steel doorknob, Azzedine Alaia, Paris, designed by Écart (showroom not shown in this book).

Folding screen for the dressing rooms of Azzedine Alaïa, designed by Écart and made of a chrome structure, a mirror, and a metal "mosquito net" (showroom not shown in this book).

Desk and chair, Ebel, made of pickled white oak with the central surface in frosted glass.

Chair for the Issey Miyake showroom designed by Shiro Kuramata in metal meshing and chrome-plated steel with a seat of colored leather. Manufactured by Vitra.

Clothing rack, Esprit, Cologne, made of pastel-printed plastic laminate.

ITALY 1976
Missoni.
Wool clothing for men and women.
Via Montenapoleone, Milan.
Architects: Gregotti Associates, Milan.
The showroom's cubic volume is cut diagonal-
ly by a staircase whose footprint is echoed on
the ground floor in a strip of carpet marking a
circulation path. The graphic nature of this ele-
ment gives the impression of a volume sus-
pended in the void. Because space was
limited, the architects deftly exploited its dou-
ble height, expanded in a T-form on the stairs.

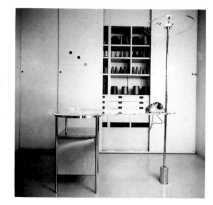

ITALY 1982
Recamificio.
Notions.
Via Bava 13, Turin.
Architects: Invenzione: Loredana
Dionigio, Marco Fatuma-Mao, Turin.
Small, perfectly cubic volume resembling
a transparent sewing box. The simple
geometric decor is composed of mag-
netic triangular or star-shaped elements
that can be moved around on the walls
and a ceiling covered with metallic panel-
ing.

AUSTRIA 1979
Reisebüro City.
Israeli Tourist Office.
Stephansplatz 10, 1010 Vienna.
Architect: Hans Hollein, Vienna.
The elongated plan consists of 154
square meters of floor area. The en-
trance area, reserved for public use, is
equipped with a continuous reception
desk typical of most tourist offices. The
concept of travel is evoked at the back of
the space by a theatrical zone with a
stone wall in ruins and palm trees in
bronze-plated brass.

ITALY 1982
Misani.
Jewelry store.
Via Montenapoleone 12, Milan.
Architects: Jonathan de Pas, Donato
d'Urbino, Paolo Lomazzi, Milan.
The interior decor consists of a few
strong elements. An enormous table
made of imitation stone extends across
the entire space, acting as a surface on
which to display jewelry as well as a
place to work and carry out sales and
transactions. The front window is viewed
through a slot cut in the stone facade.
The whole is a studied blend of natural
and artificial stone.

GREAT BRITAIN 1979
Joseph.
Men's and women's clothing.
6 Sloane Street, London SW1.
Architects: Foster Associates, London.
First Joseph showroom in London. Enor-
mous, totally hi-tech space, precursor to
the stripped-down "black and white"
style. Foster uses an industrial vocabu-
lary: a tubular structure, prefabricated
footbridges and stairways that resemble
the technical structures used in theaters.
The pirelli floor imitates that of the "glass
house." The double-height ceiling forces
the scheme's modernist character.

ITALY 1982
Buso.
Shoes.
Via Gobetti 7, Turin.
Architects: Enrico Morteo and Roberto
Vincenzi, Turin.
Homage to the great designers of the twen-
ties and thirties, based on a palette of black,
white, and chrome. The boutique, located
on the corner of one of Turin's major streets,
has two walls of windows exposing its in-
terior. The strip of light colored marble on
the floor marks a circulation path for cus-
tomers trying on shoes.

SPAIN 1982
Bis de Bis.
Women's shoes.
Galerias bulevard Rosa, paseo de
Gracia 55, Barcelona.
Architect: Eduard Samso, Barcelona.
Striking concept for the display of shoes
on metal stems that rhythmically punctu-
ate the space. Behind a facade made of
glass, the interior is conceived like a tiny
stage set. The uniform gray tinting, modu-
lated by spot lighting, highlights the
touches of color provided by the shoes.

ITALY 1983
Granciclismo.
Bicycle equipment.
Via Folli 43, Milan.
Architects: Daniela Puppa and Franco
Raggi, Milan.
Lighting: Piero Castiglioni.
This shop, devoted to bicycles and cycling
equipment, also houses a library and video
room. The space is divided into several
zones of which the main axis is an inclined
test track. The specially designed furniture
on wheels is painted in the colors of the
Italian flag.

ITALY 1984
Knoll International.
Showroom for contemporary furniture.
Via Montenapoleone, Milan.
Architect: Cini Boeri, Milan.
Renovation of six floors of a registered building. The large glass panels of the display
window run behind the stone facade, which
maintains its original character. The interior
design is minimalist and strictly modern.
Polished black granite slabs cover the entire
floor on the street level, and the walls are
painted quiet shades of white and pale gray.
Knoll's classic designs are displayed on a
half-height mezzanine without railings.

FRANCE 1985
Galerie Yves Gastou.
Twentieth-century decorative arts.
12, rue Bonaparte, Paris.
Architect: Sottsass Associates, Milan.
Gallery for designer objects and furniture
from the 1930's to today. Small, L-
shaped space lit in the back by a large
skylight and elsewhere by a series of adjustable spots. The floor is made of pink-
tinted and matte-finished wood (by
Sottsass's special method). The black
and white granito facade nods to the fifties, Gastou's specialty.

ITALY 1984
Macatre.
Office furniture showroom.
Via Manzoni 12, Milan.
Architects: Perry A. King and Santiago
Miranda, Milan.
Sales and display space on three levels,
one of which is the basement. The spa-
cious entrance hall has a double-height
ceiling. A great effort was expended in
selecting materials and designing
details. The floor is of polished black
granite. The white marble stairs and land-
ing are offset by the black of the metal
railings and baseboards.

FRANCE 1985
Tokyo Kumagaï.
Shoes.
33, rue Saint-Guillaume, Paris.
Architects: Kazutoshi Morita and Pierre
du Besset, Paris.
The entrance is on the corner of an old
stone building. The ground floor space is
composed of functional elements: a frosted
glass screen, a projecting steel cashier's
desk, a curved partition in sandblasted
glass, and a suspended beam used for
hanging clothes. The designers chose
wood and marble as opposed to oxi-
dized metal or splintered stone furniture.

ITALY 1984
Zeus.
Men's and women's clothing, design (objects, furniture), and exhibition space.
Via Vigevano 8, Milan.
Architect: Maurizio Peregalli, Milan.
Space of 150 square meters in the heart of
old Milan, in a building that had been entirely renovated. Both gallery and shop are
done in the eighties style: minimalist spaces
with polished concrete floors, white painted
walls, halogen lighting, glass partitions with
black metal fixtures. The clothing shop is
visible from the street, whereas the design
gallery circumscribes an interior courtyard.

FRANCE 1985
Christophe Lebourg.
Men's and women's clothing.
Rue Étienne-Marcel, Paris.
Architects: Asymétrie: Bernard Fric and
Dominique Kelly, Paris.
The architects defined an entrance axis
angled off the street. The scheme
evokes a series of continuous move-
ments and tensions, from the large panels of sandblasted glass used in the front
window displays to the lights suspended
from metal cables to the steel plates (of
the racks and shelves) that take up the
curved forms of the partition.

HONG KONG 1984
Esprit.
Clothing and accessories.
Architect: Shiro Kuramata, Tokyo.
Enormous four-story space with grilling
on the walls and ceiling resembling a
large metal cage. This functional design
element serves to support the lighting fixtures and racks and cubbyholes for clothing, shoes, and accessories. The ground
floor evokes the atmosphere of a railway
station hall with its numbered compart-
ments and its curved volume made of
aluminum sheeting.

FRANCE 1985
Marithé et François Girbaud.
Men's and women's clothing.
38, rue Étienne-Marcel, Paris.
Architects: Antonia Astori (Milan) and
Michel Hamon (Paris).
The showroom is characterized by a
spectacular facade, glazed on three
floors, behind which unfolds an enormous staircase. Inside, the space nar-
rows but the spectacle continues at the
cashier's corner, with its curved
aluminum wall of videos. Neon lighting
lends a bluish, chilly atmosphere.

Jouets & Co. Showroom.

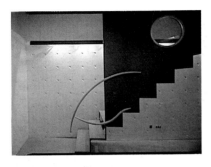

ITALY 1985
BP Studio.
Men's and women's clothing.
Florence.
Architect: Claudio Nardi, Florence.
Narrow shop of 75 square meters on
three levels. The effect of depth has
been exaggerated by inserting an ethereal staircase that unifies the whole by
means of a play of lights and transparencies. The partitions along the staircase
are decorated plaster panels. The
strange character of this space is due
to its subtle mix of art deco and exotic
references.

FRANCE 1986
Irie.
Women's clothing.
10, rue du Pré-aux-Clercs, Paris.
Architect: Denis Colomb.
Intimate boutique with a front window exposing the clothing within rather than a
true display window. The space is im-
maculate white with a marble floor. It
seems as private in its decor as in its
spatial configuration. The whole is
stripped down and filled with exotic elements implying a scenario other than
that of sales: a stuffed tiger, a piano, a
400-kilo alabaster basin.

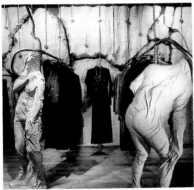

GREAT BRITAIN 1985
Bazaar.
Clothing.
London.
Architect: Ron Arad, London.
The showroom no longer exists, but it
deserves mention because of the excite-
ment generated by its opening. It seemed
to stress a mood of "no future," with its
mummified bodies recalling Pompeii. The
materials—wood floors, engraved mirrors,
halogen tubes—were for the most part sal-
vaged debris and atypical, reinforcing the
disquieting atmosphere.

FRANCE 1986
Jouets & Cie.
Self-service toy store.
11, boulevard de Sébastopol, Paris.
Architect: Philippe Starck-Monfort-Lamaury.
The space is characterized primarily by
its impressive front window, in which no
toys are displayed. The only thing seen
here is a gigantic doll facing directly
toward the street. Behind this window,
conceived as a screen, a large curved
wall surrounds this enormous, solitary
actor. The surprise effect is increased by
the fact that both doll and wall are
painted gold.

UNITED STATES 1985
Esprit.
Clothing and accessories.
Los Angeles.
Architect: Joe d'Urso, New York.
Conceived as a clothing supermarket,
the space is as extensive in height as in
floor area. The black metal superstruc-
ture on which are attached cinema spotlights, the crowding of display elements,
the colors, the personalized furniture,
and the footbridges make one think of an
enormous spinning surface on which customers and vendors are the actors.

FRANCE 1986
Equipment.
Men's shirts.
46, rue Etienne-Marcel, Paris.
Architects: David Chipperfield Assoc., London.
Successful example of the possibility of
designing a space of merely 15 square
meters. The showroom is at the same
time one big display window and a sales
area. The primary material is wood, used
for the floor and for the partition that
serves as a place to display and organize
goods. The architects chose contrasting
colors: pale green for the walls, carmine
red for the dressing room curtains.

JAPAN 1985
Inoue sacs.
Leather goods and handbags.
Takashimaya Plaza, 1-12 Sennichi-cho,
Kagoshima City.
Architect: Masaki Morita, Tokyo.
Geometric space punctuated by display
shelves for products. The perfectly symmetrical design is interrupted by a symbolic intervention: an enormous striped
crayon-shaped volume descending head
first from the ceiling toward the floor. It
symbolizes a volcanic eruption that oc-
curred in Kagoshima.

SPAIN 1986
Teresa Ramallal.
Clothing, shoes, and accessories.
Calle Almirante 7, Madrid.
Architect: Tonet Sunyer, Barcelona.
The double facade maintains the previous look of the space. It consists of a
double portico with a curved wall of slid-
ing glass panels behind. The elongated
interior space is divided into two parts by
frosted glass screens. The shoe corner
is distinctive—a wall of illuminated
square niches containing display models.

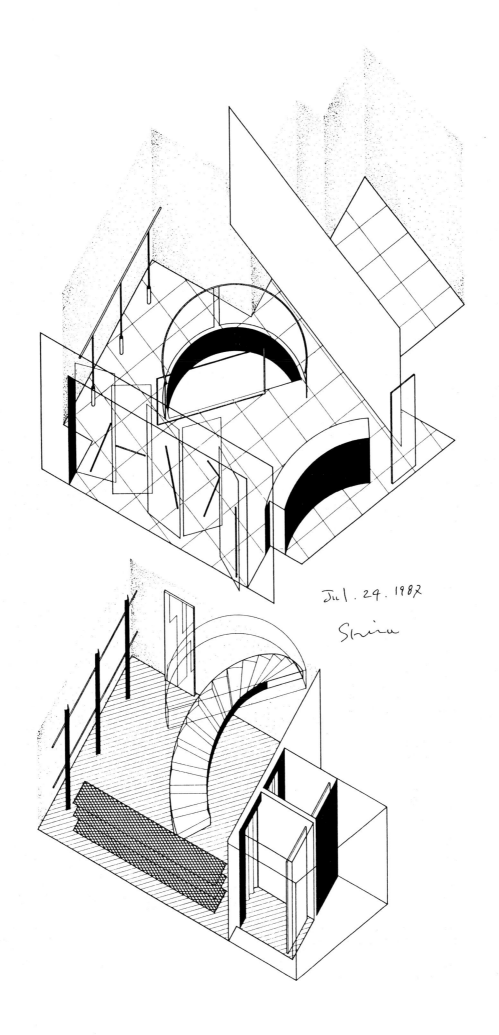

Jul. 24. 1982

Shira

Issey Miyake Showroom.

UNITED STATES 1986
Parachute, Soho.
Men's and women's ready-to-wear clothing.
121 Wooster Street, New York.
Architect: Harry Parnass, Québec.
Typical New York conversion of an industrial space into a commercial loft. The ground floor of the enormous shop is divided in two. There is also a vast basement area below. The metal structure of the building was kept. The columns are cast iron, the ceiling pressed tin, and the walls and floors unfinished concrete. Clothing is displayed on large, sloped expanses of concrete and on simple metal racks.

FRANCE 1987
Williwear Willismith.
Men's and women's clothing.
92, rue de Richelieu, Paris.
Architect: Dan Friedman, New York.
Two distinct yet adjacent spaces, one for men and one for women. The stripped-down space is characterized by its personalized furniture. A sea-green wall remains in its rough state as a relic of the existing space. The fluorescent orange plastic doors of the dressing rooms are quilted. The curved plaster ceiling is entirely luminous. The cashier's desk, a sculpture in its own right, lords over the middle of the room.

JAPAN 1986
Season's Gallery.
Men's and women's clothing.
Komatsu Building, Ginza, Tokyo.
Architect: Marie-Christine Dorner, Paris.
Boutique inserted in a Japanese department store. Very elegant method of playing with tensions and torsions. The wall seen here traces in its length the pattern of a sheet of paper whose tension is gradually shifted from one side to the other. The whole scheme is an exploration of the density of lines and materials.

ITALY 1987
Officina Alessi.
High design housewares.
Corso Matteoti 9, Milan.
Architect: Sottsass Associates, Milan.
Coffee makers by Aldo Rossi and Dalisi, tea kettles by Michael Graves and Sapper, objects by Sottsass, Mendini, etc., are now on view in one place—170 square meters on three levels. The space is characterized by great attention to materials: Canadian granito, synthetic marmorino, and pink and black marble. The entrance in the front glass window is marked by a polished red and yellow metal door.

FRANCE 1987
Alain Mikli.
Eyeglasses and optics.
1, rue des Rosiers, Paris.
Architect: Jacques Dagnot, Paris.
Original idea for the display and sale of eyeglasses. The space is divided into several corners arranged like small salons. Everything is designed in curved lines, from the walls and furniture to the illuminated installations that trace the sinuous line of the plasterwork. The entrance door, in solid light wood, is remarkable; concave in form, it is pierced by a large pair of opera glasses.

THE NETHERLANDS 1987
Esprit Benelux.
Men's and women's clothing.
Spui 10, 1012 Amsterdam WZ.
Architect: Antonio Citterio, Milan.
A building dating from the nineteenth century was renovated and converted into a headquarters, showroom, and cafe for Esprit. The hi-tech character of the materials (zinc, aluminum, varnished metal) contrasts with the wide floor-boards. The metal staircase, the core of the project, connects several levels. Located beneath a skylight, it also creates an interesting light well.

FRANCE 1987
Issey Miyake.
Men's clothing.
33, boulevard Raspail, Paris.
Architect: Shiro Kuramata, Tokyo.
Tiny boutique on two floors with little clothing on display. It is composed of transparencies and reflections in a range of neutral shades. The beautiful materials reveal the elements of the space—its volumes and surfaces. The floor is made of slabs of polished black granite, the staircase railing of cracked glass. By not including a front display window, the space is enlarged and interior and exterior are fused.

UNITED STATES 1988
Mercedes-Benz.
Automobile Showroom.
Inglewood, New Jersey.
Architect: Emilio Ambasz, New York.
This showroom for new automobiles consists of three floors inserted on a small piece of land. In order to conceal the unattractive surroundings, an enormous black marble wall rises behind the exhibition space, the floor of which undulates like a hillside to suggest movement and speed. The showroom is constructed of prefabricated concrete slabs and glass blocks.

BIBLIOGRAPHY

BOOKS

Annual of Display and Commercial Space Design in Japan, vol. 14. Tokyo, 1987.

Interiors of Uchida Mitsuhashi and Studio 80. Tokyo: Rikuyo Sha, 1987.

Le Décor des boutiques parisiennes, collective work presented by the Délégation à l'action artistique de la Ville de Paris, 1987.

Les Cahiers du CCI, "Monuments éphémères," no. 3. Paris: éditions du Centre Georges-Pompidou/CCI, 1987.

Nouvelles Tendances: les avant-gardes de la fin du XXe siècle, catalogue of the CCI exhibition. Paris: éditions du Centre Georges-Pompidou/CCI, 1987.

Hans Hollein. Métaphore et métamorphoses, catalogue of the Centre Georges-Pompidou exhibition. Paris: éditions du Centre Georges-Pompidou/CCI, 1987.

de Bure, Gilles. *Ettore Sottsass Jr.* Paris: Rivages, 1987.

Renaud, Philippe. *Starck Mobilier*, Coll. "Premier Étage." Marseilles: Ed. Michel Aveline, 1987.

Ragot, Gilles and Mathilde Dion. *Le Corbusier en France*. Paris: Electa Moniteur, 1987. (Project for Jean Bat'a, pp. 11, 12, 70, 126, 184, 195.)

Barré, Arlette. *l'UAM*. Paris: Éditions du Regard, 1987.

Catalogues Cassina. Milan: 1985, 1987.

Les Cahiers de la recherche architecturale. Carlo Scarpa. Marseilles: Parantheses, 1986.

Anargyros, Sophie. *le Style des années 80*. Paris: Rivages, 1986.

Vellay, Marc. *Pierre Chareau. Architecte-meublier 1883–1950*. Paris: Rivages, 1986.

Cabanne, Pierre. *Encyclopédie Art déco*. Paris: Somogy, 1986.

Les Cahiers du CCI, no. 2. Paris: éditions du Centre Georges-Pompidou/CCI,1986.

Biennale de Paris. Architecture, exhibition catalogue. Liège: Ed. Pierre Mardaga, 1985.

Adolf Loos. Liège: Ed. Pierre Mardaga, 1985.

Tadao Ando. Coll. "Monographies." Paris: Electa Moniteur, 1985.

Carlo Scarpa 1906–1978. Trans. from the Italian by Jean-Georges d'Hoste and Fabio Palmiri. Paris: Electa Moniteur, 1985.

Colin, Christine. *Kagu: Mobilier japonais*. Catalogue of the musee d'Angers exhibition, 1985.

Castelli, Clino Trini. *Il Lingotto primario. Progetti di design primario alla Domus Academy*. Milan: Arcadia Edizioni, 1985.

"De Stijl et l'architecture en France," catalogue of exhibition organized by the Direction de l'architecture et de l'urbanisme et l'IFA. Liège: Ed. Pierre Mardaga, 1985.

Interior Design in Japan. Tokyo: Kodansha, 1984.

Branzi, Andrea. *le Design italien. La Casa Calda*. Paris: éditions de l'Equerre, 1984.

Radice, Barbara. *Memphis*. Milan: Electa, 1984.

Memphis: The New International Style. Milan: Electa, 1981.

Gropius, Walter. *Architectures en Allemagne*. 1900–1933. Paris: éditions du CCI, 1980.

Valéry, Paul. *Eupalinos*. Paris: Gallimard, 1945, 1980.

Kron, Joan and Suzanne Slesin. *Hightech*. New York: Potter, 1978.

Calvino, Italo. *les Villes invisibles*. Les Villes et les Signes. Paris: Le Seuil, 1974.

Venturi, Robert. *l'Enseignement de Las Vegas*. Liège: Ed. Pierre Mardaga, 1974.

Barthes, Roland. *l'Empire des signes*. Skira, "Le Sentier de la création, coll. Champs." Paris: Flammarion, 1970.

L'Art décoratif d'aujourd'hui. Le Corbusier. Paris: Arthaud, 1980. (Original edition, 1925.)

JOURNALS

De Diseño, nos. 4, 8, 9, 12.

Progressive Architecture, July 1984 and January 1987.

AMC, June 1984.

L'Architecture d'aujourd'hui, "Le cas Olivetti," no. 178 (December 1976); "Design d'architectes," no. 210 (September 1980); "Projets," no. 235 (October 1984); "Habitations individuelles," no. 236 (December 1984); "OMA," no. 238 (April 1985); "Logements," no. 239 (June 1985); "Design d'interieur," no. 240 (September 1985); "Espagne," no. 245 (June 1986); "Le Corbusier," no. 249 (February 1987); "Brésil" no. 251 (June 1987); "A Paris," no. 253 (October 1987); "Ando-IMA." no. 255 (February 1988).

Architecture intérieure - Créé, (December 1982); "Le retour de la ville" (February–March 1983); (October–November 1983); "Écoles. Magasins" (June–July 1985); "Restaurants. Magasins" (October–November 1986).

Décoration internationale, January 1987.

Intramuros, no.12 (April 1987); no.15 (November 1987).

Libération, September 8, 1987, "La mode est passée, les hommes se rhabillent," pp. 34-35.

Architectural Record Interiors, 1986.

Architectural Review, no.1072 (June 1986); no.1075 (September 1986); no.1078 (December 1986); no.1089 (November 1987).

Blueprint, no. 32 (December 1986); no. 34 (February 1987); no. 35 (March 1987); no. 36 (April 1987); no. 37 (Nay 1987); no. 38 (June 1987).

Casa Vogue, October 1986, June 1987.

Domus, no. 678 (December 1986); no. 675 (September 1986); no. 688 (November 1987.

Interni, no. 338 (March 1984).

L'Espresso, September 20, 1987.

Ottagono, no. 85 (June 1987).

A + U, "Hans Hollein," 1985.

PHOTOGRAPHY CREDITS: Aldo Ballo: pp. 27–31. Gabriele Basilico: pp. 11–17. François Bergeret: pp. 67-69. Richard Bryant: pp. 89-93. Santi Caleca: pp. 23–25. Lluis Casals: pp. 35–37. Stéphane Couturier: pp. 56 (1), 57, 59–61, 75–79. Ferran Freixa: pp. 32–33. Cary Hazlegrove: p. 39. Hiroyuki Hirai: pp. 101–5. Alastair Hunter: pp. 81–83. The Japan Architect: pp. 43–45. T. Nakasa & Partners: pp. 105–9. Deidi von Schaewen: pp. 51–53. Dorotea Schwarhaupt: pp. 55, 56 (2,3). Andreas Sterzing: p. 99. Gerald Zugman: pp. 47–49. T.D.R.: pp. 63–65, 95–97.

A Technical Issue: pp. 110–11. Gerald Zugman, Carlo Orsi, Andreas Sterzing, Stéphane Couturier, Alastair Hunter, Gabriele Basilico, Ferran Freixa, Patricia Canino, Deidi von Schaewen, Hiroyuki Hirai, Aldo Ballo.

Visual Overview: p. 112, Gabriele Basilico, Gerald Zugman, Norman Foster, Jordi Sarra, Studio Azzuro, Miro Zagnoli; p. 113, Mario Carrieri, Santi Caleca, Godeaut, François Bergeret, Stéphane Couturier; p. 115, Aldo Ballo, T. Nakasa & Partners, Stéphane Couturier; p. 117, Stéphane Couturier, Isabelle Allégret, Armin Linke, Santi Caleca, Louis Checkman.